YOU CAN WHITTLE AND CARVE

YOU CAN

WHITTLE
and CARVE

By AMANDA WATKINS HELLUM

and FRANKLIN H. GOTTSHALL

BONANZA BOOKS • NEW YORK

ISBN: 517034441

© MCMXLII By The Bruce Publishing Company

This edition published by Bonanza Books,
a division of Crown Publishers, Inc.,
by arrangement with the authors

(M)

In tribute to the memory of MARTHA BERRY, Foundress of The Berry Schools, the authors dedicate this book. It deals but with the shaping of dull, common, and ordinary things into objects of interest and value; but her hands molded a far more precious raw material, enriching and transforming the lives of thousands, so that they in turn might enrich and transform the lives of countless thousands more.

FOREWORD

MANY people have an instinctive desire to carve. Especially is this true of young people. It our readers do not believe this, then a trip through the rooms and halls of almost any school building in this great land of ours should convince them of this fact. The initials carved on the desks, the marks on the furniture, the pair of hearts carved on the bark of the shade tree of the playground, all attest the fact that the younger generation likes to carve.

Many never entirely lose their desire to shape something from a piece of wood. The idler sitting on the curb, whittling a stick with his pocketknife is indulging his innate desire to carve. And many people do carve, some aimlessly, like the children who mutilate public property, or like the idler cutting shavings from a stick. Others, however (and their number is legion), actually carve something, like the sportsman friend of one of the authors, who carves his gunstocks with emblems derived from American Indian lore.

One is never too young to learn, it seems, for Junior, who just recently turned seven, has just whittled a piece of pine into something which actually resembles a horse. Nor is the desire to carve dimmed with the passing years, for many devotees of the craft have long since passed three score and ten.

Carving is an enjoyable pastime. It can become an absorbing hobby, and in many instances has developed into a profitable occupation. The boy who carves his initials on the school desk can, with the proper direction and encouragement, be changed from a despoiler of public property into an enthusiastic young sculptor. The more mature idler, under tactful impulsion, might turn his pastime into more useful channels which could lead to a profitable occupation.

Access to a book like ours, it is hoped, will kindle the spark of enthusiasm, or initiate the impulse needed to light and feed the fire of creative endeavor in this absorbing hobby. With that hope, the authors respectfully submit to the appraisal of the public these examples of work which have been turned out under their direction. The authors wish to thank student whittlers of the Berry Schools for their cheerful cooperation in posing for photographs, for help in the preparation and execution of the objects shown, and for valuable help in various other aspects of the work.

FRANKLIN H. GOTTSHALL

AMANDA WATKINS HELLUM

THE BERRY SCHOOLS, MT. BERRY, GA.

CONTENTS

CHAPTER 1

TOOLS

MANY who contemplate carving as a hobby allow their original enthusiasm to be cooled when confronted by the imposing array of tools composing the kit of the professional wood carver. Even a comparatively modestly priced set, such as the one shown in Figure 1, would make many who have the urge and the ability to carve hesitate for a long time before investing in such a set of tools.

At the very outset, then, permit us to assure the prospective wood carver that it is quite unlikely that he will need such a set of tools; and that it is almost as likely that he may already own most, if not all, of the essential tools needed to duplicate every one of the carvings which are reproduced in the following pages.

"But," says the unbelieving novice, "every book, or magazine article on wood carving I have ever read, shows an imposing array of tools, and convinces me that a set of razor-sharp chisels of various shapes is absolutely essential for success. I have none of these, nor can I afford them; at least not until I am assured of

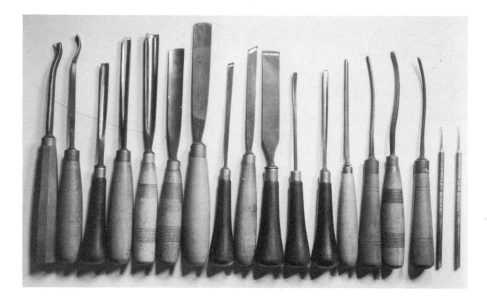

Fig. 1. A set of carving tools

the fact that I will be able to turn out reasonably satisfactory work. Without them how can I carve? One must have the tools to carve."

The answer is a simple one. Show us the person who owns one good pocket-knife, and who is possessed of a genuine desire to carve, and you will behold a wood carver in the making. Not only can the carvings, reproduced in the frontispiece, be duplicated with ordinary pocket-knives, but practically all of them have been carved with pocketknives. Many children and grownups with no previous experience have attained a great deal of skill in this absorbing craft in a remarkably short time.

It would be absurd to pretend that everyone can learn to carve. But nearly every beginner who has the urge to carve can duplicate at least some of the intriguingly beautiful examples shown in the following pages.

An assortment of wood-carving chisels, clamps, a vise, a sharpening stone, and a good workbench are desirable and helpful; but only a sharp pocketknife, or two, and a small oilstone are essential. Having this essential equipment and a soft pine block, cut to a contour roughly resembling the outline, the carver will be ready to begin. This block of pine, or other wood, known as a blank, will approximate the shape and thickness of the completed figure, though it will of necessity be slightly larger in every direction, see A, Figure 2. As for a workshop, it may be the kitchen table, or a camp chair under the most convenient shade tree.

In looking through these pages, the

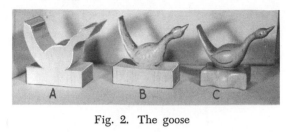
Fig. 2. The goose

prospective carver may decide that he will want to carve one of the more difficult pieces, such as the good St. Francis, shown in Figure 85. With this in mind, he may provide himself with the necessary material and equipment and, falling into the most convenient easy chair, proceed to his self-appointed task. Alas! After assiduously working for an hour or so, he is shocked to find that what he holds in his hand does not even remotely resemble the saint, and what is worse, the bird in the saint's hand has, by some mischance, found its way into the pile of chips on the floor. Possibly his arm is not properly placed and other details are poorly proportioned; so that the good fellow more nearly resembles a prize fighter than a saint, and a badly battered, bloody prize fighter into the bargain! For, the wood is not easily cut because the knife is too dull, and the ambitious novice has sustained a cut finger because of inadequate preparation.

Now, it's nice to whittle with a purpose; much nicer than it is to just whittle a stick for the pleasure of whittling, with nothing more to show for the effort than a pile of shavings. And we all long to do the unusual things; like the boy who thinks he'd like to build a desk as his first project in manual-training class. But, if a person has

2

never carved before, and knows little or nothing about achieving proper form and contour, he should first attempt only simple objects.

Almost any student or homecraftsman can carve the goose, Figure 2, and having succeeded with a carving of this type, confidence will be acquired to try something a little more difficult the next time. Furthermore (and just as important), the proper method of handling a knife will be learned, and a great deal about the limitations and peculiarities of the materials which are being used.

Since the pocketknife, sharpening stone, and a wooden blank are the minimum essentials, let us consider for a moment this most versatile of all carving tools, the knife.

In Figure 3 are shown three knives, representing the most popular types used to carve the figures in this book. It is quite possible to make one knife do for many of the simple types of work. The important thing is to have one with good steel, properly tempered, so that it will hold a razor-sharp edge. Cheap knives have coarse-grained steel which cannot be properly tempered. On such a knife it is difficult to get a keen edge and impossible to keep one. Some knives have too hard a

temper, causing the edge to break away and become saw-toothed. On others the temper is not hard enough, causing the newly sharpened edge to turn, or quickly wear away and become blunt. The knife should be well made and properly tempered. It may have as many as three or even four blades.

Some carvers prefer to use sloyd knives, on which the blade is rigidly fixed to the handle instead of being hinged like the blades on a pocketknife. Two types of sloyd knives are shown in Figure 4.

A fairly large blade will be required for heavy cutting, or boasting-in the carving. By boasting-in, we mean the rough preliminary cutting which the carver must do in order to achieve the rough form of the figure he is attempting to reproduce, see B, Figure 61.

When boasting-in a carving with a knife, the wood carver cuts both toward and away from himself, the direction of the cut depending upon the direction of the grain and the ease with which the chips may be removed by cutting in that particular direction. In Figure 5 is shown the method of holding the block when the cut is toward you. Figure 6 shows the proper way to hold the work when the cut is away from you. Endeavor always to

Fig. 3. Popular types of knives

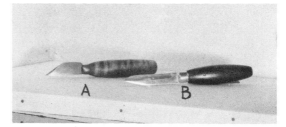

Fig. 4. Sloyd knives

3

Fig. 5. Method of holding block when cutting toward you

Fig. 6. Method of holding block when cutting way from you

nose, and other heavy cutting designed to remove excess wood. For preliminary steps such as this, a fairly wide, heavy spear-point blade will be needed, Figure 10, which will permit the removal of wide thick chips at every cut. Some carvings are never carried much beyond the boasting-in stage, shown in *A*, Figure 9, while others are carefully smoothed, and have

hold the work firmly, but with the fingers in such a position that, should the knife slip, it will not cut them.

On flat work, shown in Figure 7, the boasting-in will consist of rounding off sharp edges, correcting faulty outlines, which may appear in the blank as a result of the band sawing, and lowering backgrounds surrounding sharply defined outlines, such as the ears and necklines of the dogs.

In carving figures such as the mule-head book ends, shown in Figure 8, boasting-in will consist of cutting away excess stock between the ears, rounding the edges along the neck, forehead, and

Fig. 7. The dogs

Fig. 8. Carved figures

hairlines cut to register the minutest details. Even though it is planned to complete the carving with bold, broad strokes of the knife, each finishing cut must be carefully executed, so that the completed figure will definitely resemble the thing it is supposed to represent.

In most instances the carver will wish to complete his figure to the minutest detail. After he has achieved the rough contour, exemplified by *A*, Figure 9, he will want to begin smoothing out the rough waves and sharp angles left by the broad blade of the heavy cutting tool. For this operation, a clip blade, shaped somewhat like the one shown in Figure 11 will be found useful. This medium-sized blade, with its long-sloped curve on the end, is perfect for smoothing rough spots, since it is ideally shaped for a slicing, rather than a shearing cut.

For the final cutting, where a great deal of detailing is to be done, such as cutting the mane of the horse, *B*, Figure 9, or the eyes of the rabbit, Figure 14, a small, thin blade with a very sharp point, known

Fig. 9. Horses and mule

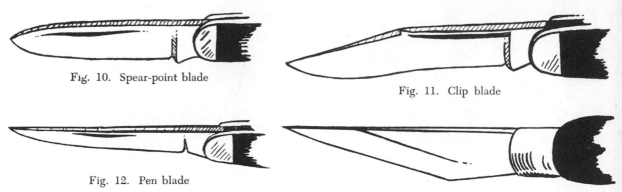

Fig. 10. Spear-point blade

Fig. 11. Clip blade

Fig. 12. Pen blade

Fig. 13. Skew-edged blade

as a pen blade, Figure 12, will be needed. With this knife, very small chips, such as those necessary to carve eyes or nostril holes, may be cut out.

The types of blades preferred by various wood carvers will vary, since everyone who carves will become attached to one type or another in the course of time. The skew-edged blade shown in Figure 13, for example, will serve to do all of the delicate cutting for which the thin, slender blade shown in Figure 12 is intended. This shape is also best adapted to do chip carving, when triangular-shaped chips are cut from the wood to form the pattern. A knife of this type with a fixed blade, a favorite of one of the authors, is also shown at A, in Figure 4.

The most important thing, next to the knife itself, is the means of keeping it sharp. For this, three things are necessary: (1) a fine-grit emery wheel, Figure 15, (2) a fine-grit India oilstone, B, Figure 16, and (3) a piece of leather dressed with fine emery paste, to be used as a stropping tool, C, Figure 16.

If a grinder, powered by an electric motor, is not available, then a hand-powered

grinder will do. The grinder, fitted with a fine-grit emery wheel, is used to thin out the blunt edges of blades on new and old knives, in preparation for honing. The cutting edges of new blades will always need thinning, since the knife is never sharpened at the factory. Old blades become blunt with use, and constant honing on the oilstone tends to shorten the bevel of the cutting edge, making regrinding necessary.

It is possible to keep knives sharp by means of the oilstone alone. Patience and

Fig. 14. Carving eyes on rabbit with point of knife

6

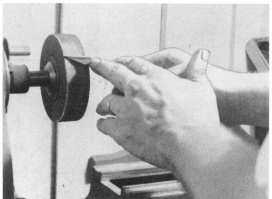

Fig. 15. Knife being ground on a fine emery wheel

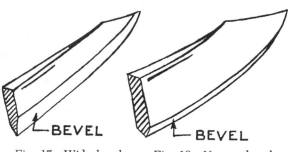

Fig. 17. Wide bevel   Fig. 18. Narrow bevel

persistence will accomplish almost any- thing. But, if a great deal of carving is going to be done, a grinder will be almost indispensable.

An electric-powered grinder is prefer- able, because it leaves both hands free to hold the knife while it is being ground. The edge of the blade is held horizontally, so that the stone rotates toward the edge. Since the emery wheel revolves quite rap- idly, the blade must be kept in constant motion from side to side, so as to avoid burning the steel, thus drawing its temper.

The steel should never be allowed to be- come hot, but should be frequently dipped into a conveniently placed can of water whenever it feels uncomfortably warm to the touch. If the blade is pressed lightly against the wheel and kept in constant motion by deft manipulation over the stone, it can be ground to the proper thin- ness without harm.

To be properly ground, the bevel on the edge of the blade should be quite wide, like the one shown in Figure 17, rather than with a narrow bevel, shown in Figure 18. The first blade cuts easily, because the wood offers very little resist- ance to the acute-angled, V-shaped bevel.

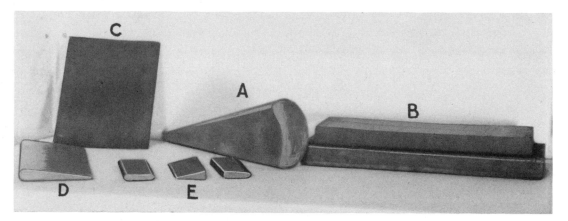

Fig. 16. Honing stones. A, Gouge slip; B, fine-grit India oilstone; C, stropping tool; D, oilstone; E, small slips

7

The edge of the blade shown in Figure 18 may be just as sharp as the edge of the other one, but because of its short, wide-angled bevel, it meets with more resistance when it enters the wood. The first blade may also be held at a more advantageous angle, permitting one to slice away very thin chips. A blade sharpened like the second one would have to be held so nearly perpendicular to the block of wood in order to start the cut, that carving with it would prove awkward if not impossible.

All sharpening operations wear away part of the steel edge on a knife blade or chisel. The emery wheel wears the edge away very rapidly and the result is a rough-cutting edge. Thus, if one were to look at such an edge through a magnifying glass, it would resemble the teeth on a saw. Furthermore, this rough edge is not hard or firm enough to overcome the resistance to sever the fibers of the wood. The paper-thin, saw-toothed edge will break away when brought into contact with the wood. Consequently a finer abrasive tool must be used to hone away the infirm particles of steel, known to every woodworker as the wire edge. A fine-grit India oilstone will do this. India oilstones are classified as coarse, medium, and fine; and only the last will be suitable to sharpen wood-carving tools.

To sharpen the blade on an India oilstone, mix equal parts of light machine oil and kerosene, and spread a few drops of this mixture over the surface of the stone. Then lay the blade to be sharpened nearly flat upon the stone and begin honing it by rubbing it firmly over the entire surface

Fig. 19. Whetting the knife on the oilstone

of the stone with a circular motion, Figure 19. Frequently alternate from one side of the blade to the other so as to entirely remove the wire edge. If the blade has good steel you will get a firm, smooth, keen edge which will stay sharp, even though it is subjected to considerable use.

Many carry the sharpening process no further than this. A still keener cutting edge can be obtained by stropping the blade on a piece of leather which has been treated with a coat of fine emery paste, or valve-grinding compound. This further smoothes out the sawlike teeth which will be found on even the most carefully honed blade. One can never entirely remove these very small teeth, but carrying the sharpening process through these three operations should give a razor-sharp cutting edge.

The knife, and the tools for sharpening it, comprise the complete kit of the kind of wood carver known as the whittler. A tool kit may be kept within these limits, since nearly all of the carvings shown on the following pages were carved with nothing more. Occasionally every wood

Fig. 20. A narrow fluting tool used to trim a curve which is awkward to reach with a knife. The proper method of holding the figure and the tool

tions which are difficult to perform with a knife, Figure 20. Wood carvers who know how to use them, and who already own a good set, will prefer to do a great deal of their carving with chisels.

A fairly good collection of wood-carving tools is shown in Figure 1. The most common type is the tang chisel having the straight blade. In addition to this type there are long-bent tools, short-bent tools (the latter, if front bent, are often referred to as "spoons"). Short-bent tools are either front bent or back bent.

Most of the time, straight tools are used for heavy cutting. They may be either hammered into the wood with a wooden

carver will find it advantageous to use one or more wood-carver's chisels. These chisels permit easier access to places difficult to get at. They also facilitate cutting opera-

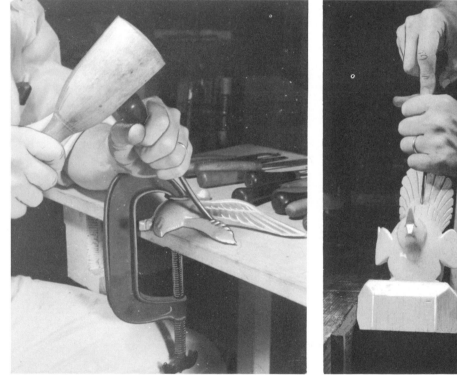

Fig. 21. Carving chisel hammered with a mallet

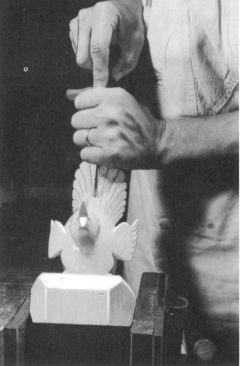

Fig. 22. Left hand guides and controls the chisel while the right furnishes the power to push it through the wood

9

mallet, as shown in Figure 21, or merely pushed along with the hand, as shown in Figure 22. Straight and bent tools are made with three main types of cutting edges known as chisels, gouges, and V tools.

Chisels are sharpened straight across the blade, or on the skew; that is, the sharpened end makes an angle of from 45 to 60 deg. with the blade. Not only is the chisel thinner and lighter than the carpenter's chisel, but the cutting edge is beveled on both sides of the blade.

U-shaped gouges are known as veiners, fluters, or deep gouges, according to their widths. Gouges under ¼ in. are veiners and those from ¼ to ½ in. are known as fluters. The curve of the cutting edge is known as the sweep of the tool. High-grade tools are usually numbered and the sweeps of straight chisels run from No. 1 in the chisels to No. 11 for the deep U-shaped tools. All sweeps come in widths varying from 1/16 to 1½ in.

The wide, shallow gouges and extra flats are used for boasting-in, for forming contours, and for lowering and smoothing open background areas.

V tools and veiners are used to outline the pattern and also to put in the delicate finishing lines which give so much character to hand-carved work. V tools are made to vary from right angles to more acute angles, and come in straight, short-bent, and long-bent tools.

Square U-shaped tools, also known as macaroni shapes, may be used to smooth backgrounds close to the outline of the

TABLE OF SWEEPS, SIZES, AND TYPES OF A FAMOUS BRAND OF SHEFFIELD STEEL CARVING TOOLS

SWEEPS 1/16" TO 1½"	NO.	NAME	LONG BENT	SPOON	BACK BENT	V-TOOLS
—	1	CHISELS		21		39 –WIDE
/	2	SKEW		22–23		40–MEDIUM
—	3	EXTRA-FLAT	12	24	33	41–NARROW
—	4	EXTRA-FLAT	13	25	34	
⌣	5	GOUGES	14	26	35	
⌣	6	GOUGES	15	27	36	
⌣	7	GOUGES	16	28	37	
⌣	8	GOUGES	17	29	38	
⌣	9	GOUGES	18	30	38	
∪	10	DEEP GOUGE	19	31	38	
∪	11	DEEP GOUGE	20	32	38	
∪	11	FLUTER				
∪	11	VEINER				

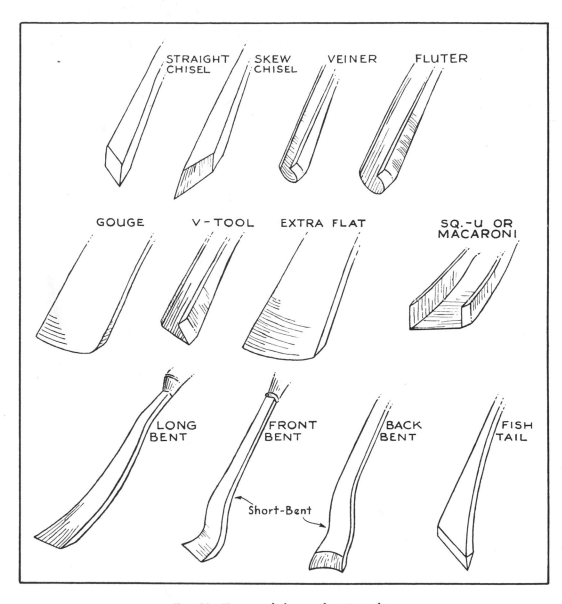

Fig. 23. Types and shapes of cutting edges

pattern. Fluters and deep U-shaped gouges are used to cut deep grooves and to trim away the wood around and inside narrow openings.

Long-bent tools, which may be had in the same sweeps as the straight tools, are not so well suited for heavy cutting or for hammering with a mallet as the straight tools; but they are unsurpassed for light cutting which may be done by pushing them along. To guide and control the tool in cutting, one grips the tool with the fingers of the left hand over the blade near the cutting end while it is being

11

pushed forward with the right hand.

Short-bent tools are a bit awkward to handle at first. One cuts with them by digging or gouging out the chips. They are used mostly to dig out or trim away acute curves in places where parts of the work obstruct normal cutting. For example, it is difficult to trim away the wood in a place like under the breast of the squirrel, Figure 59, with ordinary tools, but with a spoon it is a simple matter to do so.

The shape and type of cutting edge strongly suggests the kind of work the tool is fitted to do. The wide cutting edge of a knife must always be drawn or pushed through the wood. The chisel, which may be gripped in several different ways, has a long blade and a narrower cutting edge than the knife. It may be driven deeply into the wood with a mallet, or it may be skillfully and accurately manipulated around sharp curves and corners, Figure 24, or it may reach into deep places inaccessible to a knife blade. If the place is accessible, cutting in the round is quicker with a knife. It has the advantage of being a one-handed tool because it leaves the other hand free to hold the work. Flat work, like the plaques, is much more easily done with chisels. On flat work, the knife blade may be pushed along with the thumb of the left hand while holding on to the handle of the knife with the right hand.

The same procedure is gone through to sharpen carving chisels as to sharpen a knife. They are ground, honed, and then stropped on a piece of leather. All chisels have a longer bevel at the cutting edge

Fig. 24. A V tool being skillfully and deftly manipulated around a sharp curve using a mallet

than do knives, simply because the blades are thicker and the cutting edges narrower.

Straight chisels and skew chisels are sharpened exactly as are ordinary chisels, except that they are beveled on both sides of the blade. All other shapes, such as gouges, V tools, etc., are beveled on the outside only.

Great care must be exercised in grinding carving chisels, for the steel is much finer grained than that in ordinary woodworking chisels; and also it is not tempered as hard. While the edge may not stand

12

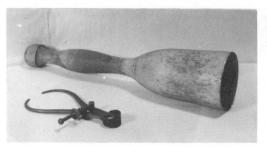

Fig. 25. Pair of calipers and a mallet

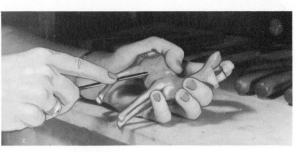

Fig. 26. Small figures in the round held in the hand

as great a shock as will the edge of an ordinary chisel, it may be given a razor-keen edge more easily. This permits the operator to make crisp, smooth cuts, entirely free of rough abrasions. In grinding a carving chisel, the tool must never be permitted to overheat, but upon becoming warm, it must quickly be dipped in water. Only very light pressure must be exerted in holding the tool against the grinding wheel, especially when the bevel is about to be brought to a wire edge. Otherwise the carbon will be burned out of the steel, resulting in loss of the temper which permits it to hold its edge.

Since there are so many oddly shaped chisels, honing stones, known as carver's "slips," are needed to remove the wire edges and burrs from the insides of the cutting tools. A collection of these is shown in Figure 16. Slips are fine India or Arkansas oilstones, shaped to fit the sharp, narrow curves and angles of the various tools. The gouge slip shown at *A*, Figure 16, is also useful in sharpening lathe tools. To bring the edges to their keenest cutting forms, they should be stropped on prepared leather.

In closing this chapter, let us call attention to one or two other tools useful

to the wood carver. In Figure 25 is shown the proper type of mallet to use for wood carving. In shape and weight it resembles the old-fashioned wooden potato masher. For light cutting, such as will be done on the type of carving in the following pages, a mallet made of hard maple or hickory, and of the size shown (2¾-in. diameter by 11 in.) will do.

If the carving is to be done with chisels, clamps and vises are useful to hold the work. In Figure 24 is shown some work held in a vise while it is being carved. If whittling with a knife, the carver may want to sit down to do his carving, but if chisels are used it will be more convenient to stand, and to have the work fastened to a workbench. A bench as high as the crooked elbow, when the carver stands upright, will be the most convenient. A regular woodworker's vise and clamps are very useful; but small figures in the round, if they are too delicate to fasten in a vise or with a clamp, must be held in the hand as in Figure 26.

A pair of calipers, Figure 25, will be useful to measure the thicknesses of wood. Measurements are made by turning the thumb nut, to adjust the jaws to the thickness you wish to determine, and then

13

Fig. 27. Sanding a carving

When sanding a carving, it should be done as shown in Figure 27. Since the sand particles left on the wood will quickly dull the tools, do no sanding until the carving has been completed.

All sanding should be done with No. 4/0 garnet paper first, and then for a final sanding, No. 6/0 garnet paper should be used. Except where sharp corners are to be preserved, the sandpaper (⅛ part or less of a standard-sized sheet) is rolled up to form a cylinder and then rubbed back and forth over the carving, as shown in Figure 27. Extremely sharp edges require little or no sanding if they have been properly cut with sharp tools.

measuring the space between the jaws with a ruler.

CHAPTER 2

WOODS SUITABLE FOR CARVING

CALIFORNIA SUGAR PINE, WHITE PINE

BECAUSE it is so easy to obtain, and because of its many other fine qualities, it would be advisable to use white pine as a first choice of material for wood carving. This is especially true if most of the carving is to be done with a knife.

White pine, especially the species known as California sugar pine, has very little grain and is entirely free of knots. The good grades are soft without having the rubber or corklike toughness so often found in sapwood of other species. The kiln-dried F.A.S. (firsts and seconds) grades of this lumber offer little resistance to a sharp-cutting tool. A sharp knife or chisel will slice or sever the fibers across the grain almost as smoothly as it will with the grain.

Being cream colored to light reddish brown in the heartwood, and running from these light hues to paler yellow and even white in the sapwood, pine is easily finished to suit almost anyone's taste.

Another great advantage pine has over other woods is that it may be bought cheaply almost anywhere where lumber is sold, and in almost any thickness or width desired. Good kiln-dried stock will remain free of checks and other defects to which many woods are subject.

California sugar pine has long brownish resin ducts, but is otherwise almost without grain figure. True northern white pine has more distinct grain markings and does not have the resin ducts, and neither does it carve quite as well as the sugar pine.

AROMATIC RED CEDAR

For those who wish to carve animals, aromatic red cedar is an excellent wood in many respects. The heartwood runs from a light red brown to purplish red in color; though these colors fade if the wood is exposed to the air and left unfinished. The sapwood runs from rich cream to white in color. Streaks of sap on the nose or tail of an animal, or down the front of a human likeness, give striking results and excellent contrast of pattern.

Knots, which are plentiful in this wood, should be scrupulously avoided when cutting out the blanks for a carving. The wood should be absolutely free from all season checks to which even well-dried wood is subject. Sometimes these do not appear to go very deep, but upon carving a piece on which they are found, what at first appeared to be merely a shallow surface crack may run as deep as ¾ in. or even deeper. If such a blank were carved it would be sure to result in an imperfect product, and the piece might even split off entirely.

Like white pine, cedar is soft, though firm under the knife, and it cuts well. It splits more readily than most woods, and on delicate members which are easily broken, the work must be very carefully handled.

MAHOGANY

There are many kinds of mahogany, and most grades are hard to surpass as carving material. Even soft grades are harder and firmer than either cedar or white pine.

The grain of mahogany is a little more coarse in texture than white pine or cedar, though never too coarse for carving purposes. Frequently the interlocked grain furnishes stock with a striped or highly figured pattern which is exceedingly pleasing on a carved figure.

The wood has remarkable color qualities, and ranges in hue from pale to deep red browns, with a rich orange undertone. Exposure to light and air darkens the wood. The texture and quality of the wood is such that transparent stains accentuate the pattern formed by the highly figured grain of the wood after finishing and polishing. Judged by every conceivable standard, mahogany is one of the very finest materials available to the wood carver.

BLACK WALNUT

Black walnut has many of the desirable qualities possessed by mahogany, though it is harder and tougher. It carves well with chisels, but is somewhat more difficult to cut with a knife. It does not split

easily, because of a firm, tough, and fibrous grain. Consequently, it is an excellent wood for carving objects on which some of the members might readily be broken or split off.

The wood is chocolate to purplish brown in color. Creamy sapwood streaks will disappear if the wood is steamed; and since kiln-dried stock is usually steamed preparatory to the drying process, good grades of the lumber should be fairly uniform in color.

Butternut, which sometimes closely resembles walnut and is often mistaken for it, is highly figured. It differs from genuine black walnut in that it is grayish brown in color, never red brown. The wood has cream-colored streaks and is a little softer than walnut.

YELLOW POPLAR

The heartwood of yellow poplar is excellent for carving. It is a little harder and firmer than pine and not quite so hard as mahogany. In color it runs from pale cream to light and even dark shades of green. Occasionally, pieces with brown, purple, or black streaks will be found.

The sapwood is not suitable for carving, being quite tough and, therefore, resisting even very sharp tools. The heartwood carves exceedingly well if kiln-dried woods are used.

The wood will take almost any kind of stain or paint, and though it has very little figure as a general rule, it has excellent color qualities when varnished or polished with wax. The grain is close for a soft-textured wood, differing greatly in this respect from mahogany, to which it offers pleasant color contrasts when the two are used in combination.

RED GUM

The heartwood of red gum carves well if kiln-dried wood is used. The sapwood often has a rubberlike toughness and carves poorly. The wood is somewhat harder than poplar, and is reddish or yellowish brown in color. It is one of the woods most likely to warp, but where small blanks are required this does not apply.

WILLOW

If you wish to carve a gray cat, a gray squirrel, or a gray mule, use willow. Well-seasoned heartwood is gray in color, streaked with cream and tan-colored markings. The wood is soft and carves beautifully (see cat in frontispiece).

MAPLE

Maple is one of the hardest domestic cabinet woods. In color it runs from pale cream to light yellowish brown. The straight-grained wood, though hard and firm, carves well if sharp tools are used. With maple it is possible to cut sharp, thin, knifelike edges, such as may be needed to carve the folds of a garment.

Bird's-eye, or wavy figured woods, are even more difficult to cut, but are exceedingly beautiful when highly polished.

OAK

Though this wood is common and has good qualities as a cabinet wood, we do not advise its use for carving any of the subjects under consideration here. It has a coarse, hard grain which is very difficult to cut.

OTHER WOODS

All the woods listed, with the exception of mahogany, are domestic. There are many other kinds of wood which will be satisfactory for carving if they are available. Among the domestic varieties we might mention apple, cherry, and pear. If properly seasoned, all carve rather well in the better grades.

Among foreign varieties suitable for carving are ebony, which is black in color, exceedingly dense, and firm in texture; teak, which resembles red gum in color but is much harder. Since these woods are not readily available to most wood carvers they will not be discussed in detail.

CHAPTER 3

WALL PLAQUES

A HAPPY relief from the conventional wall picture is an attractive wall plaque which any student or homecraftsman will enjoy carving. The grapes and the dogwood plaques are carved from solid material, that is, the design and background are all one piece. The other figures are carved separately and then fastened to a background of contrasting material, the color and texture of which are such as to form a pleasing combination. The butterfly plaque, of black walnut, differs from all the rest, in that it is pierced. Hung against an ivory or pastel-green wall, it will be a very effective bit of decoration.

The plaques shown in the illustrations were carved almost entirely with pocket-knives. They could be carved much more easily and quickly with wood-carving chisels, provided a set, such as those shown in Figure 1, were available. The particular examples shown have exceptional merit and appeal, and bear witness to the fact that the pocketknife is a versatile carving tool.

All numbers appearing on the plates indicate thicknesses in 16ths of an inch. Thus "6" indicates a thickness of ⅜ in.

The motifs, with one or two exceptions, are remarkably simple, considering the effectiveness of their decorative possibilities. In consequence they are easy to carve,

and their beautiful coloring adds to their ornamental value (see frontispiece).

Wood screws are used to fasten the carvings to their respective backgrounds. Holes are drilled and countersunk for flat-headed screws. It takes only two or three small screws to hold each figure. Thin brass hangers are tacked to the back of each plaque to hang them on the wall.

DOGS' HEADS

By far the simplest plaque to carve is the one with the dogs' heads, Figure 30. With a V tool, or by making sharp V cuts with a knife, first outline the ears and places where the one ear hangs below the

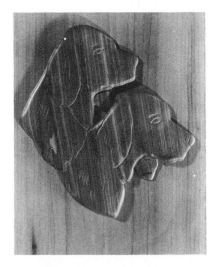

Fig. 30. Dogs' heads

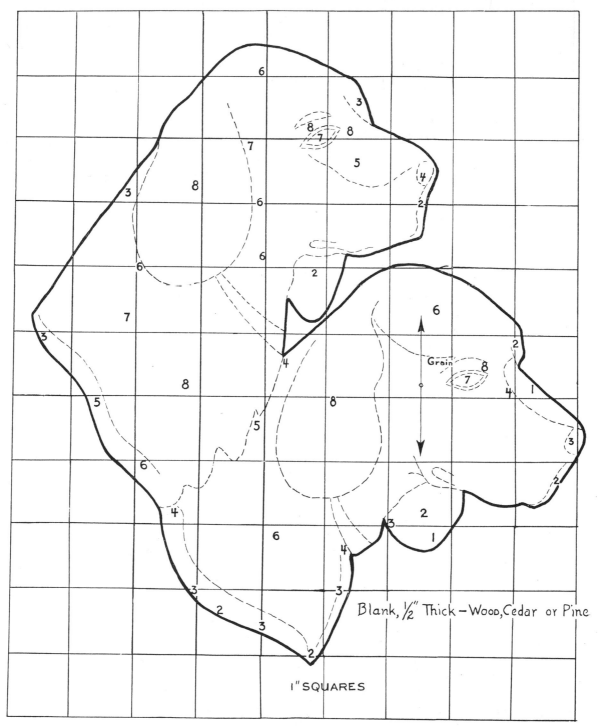

Plate 1. Dogs' heads. Note: All numbers appearing on this plate indicate thicknesses in 16ths of an inch. Thus "6" indicates a thickness of ⅜ in. This same system applies on all subsequent plates

19

Fig. 31. Flying geese

Fig. 32. Flying ducks

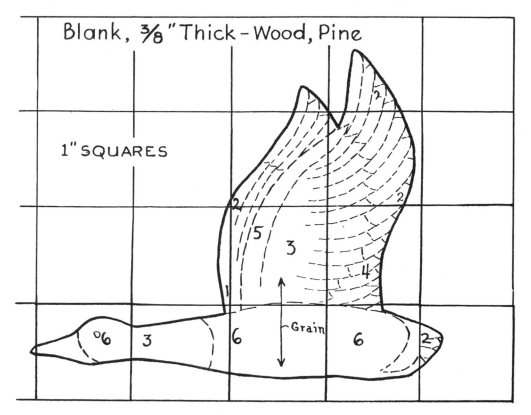

Blank, ⅜" Thick – Wood, Pine

1" SQUARES

Grain

Plate 2. Flying goose

Fig. 33. Flying Duck with a painted background

21

throat. Trim away the wood to the proper thicknesses, indicated in the drawing in Plate 1.

Next carve the eyes, first outlining them with V cuts. Trim the edges until they are well rounded, incise the hair lines, and the carving is completed.

The heads shown in Figure 30 are cedar on a 5/16 in. thick background of poplar. The heads shown in Figure 7 are painted black and are carved of white pine on a walnut background.

FLYING GEESE AND DUCKS

In so far as carving is concerned, all of the flying-geese and flying-duck plaques are similar enough to be considered together. The geese shown in Figure 31 and Plate 2 are of white pine, fastened to walnut boards.

To carve them, outline their wings with a V tool or with knife cuts. Lower the background to form the partly covered wings. With a gouge or extra-flat, cut shallow depressions on the near wing to hollow it out. Trim and round the neck, head, bill, and then the body. Cut feathers by

Fig. 34. Flying-geese plaque

making incised lines, using single sweeps of the V tool or two slices of the knife to accomplish this result.

The other plaques, shown in Figures 32 to 34 inclusive, and Plates 3, 4, and 5 are carved in the same manner, though in some instances they may entail more work than the plaque just described.

Several of the plaques are painted after they have been carved. Figure 33 has only one carved figure, the others being painted on the poplar background before waxing.

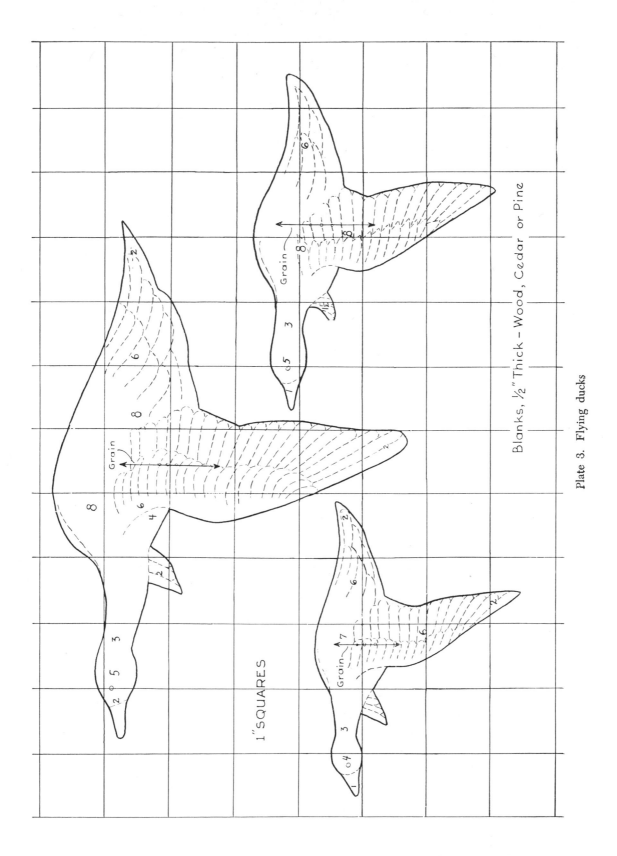

1" SQUARES

Grain

Blanks, ½" Thick – Wood, Cedar or Pine

Plate 3. Flying ducks

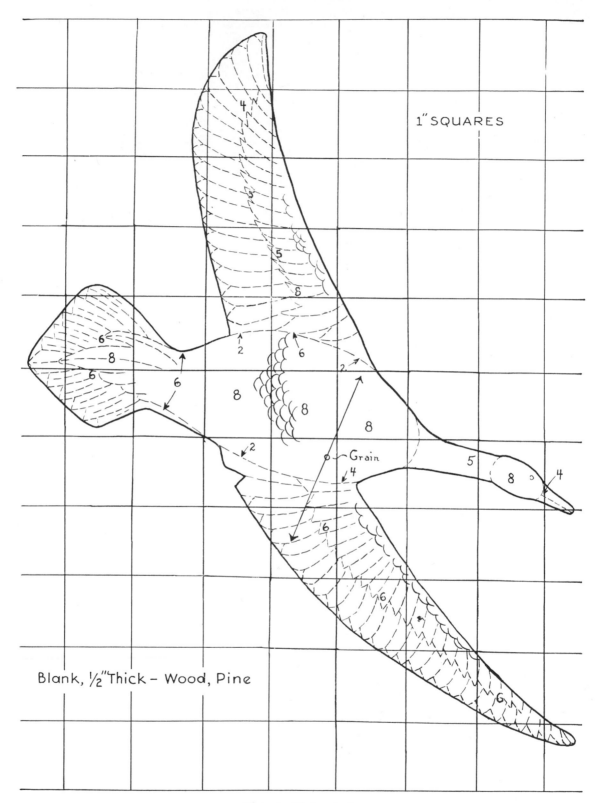

1" SQUARES

6
8
6
6
4
5
8
2
6
2
8
8
8
2
Grain
0
4
5
8
4
6
6
6

Blank, ½"Thick – Wood, Pine

Plate 4. Flying duck

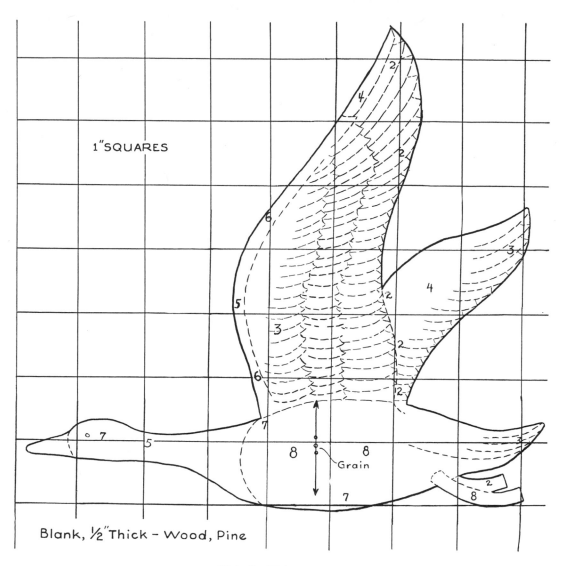

1"SQUARES

Blank, ½"Thick – Wood, Pine

Plate 5. Flying goose

25

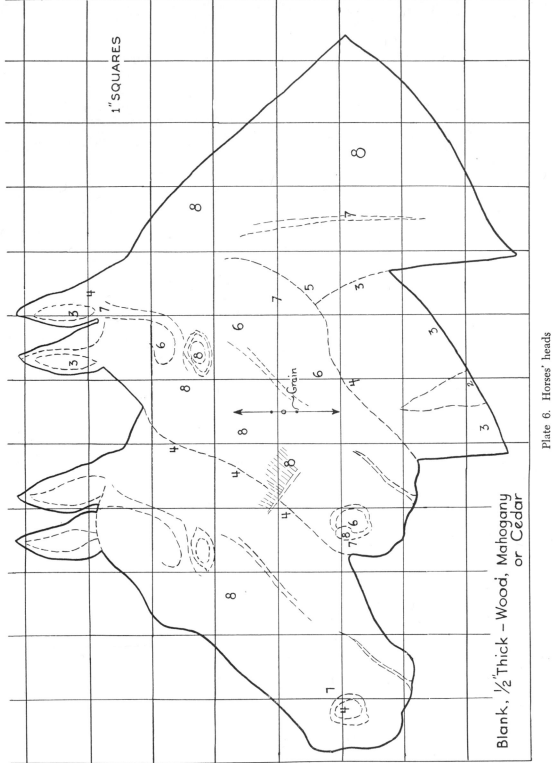

1" SQUARES

Grain

8

8

8

8

7

5

3

3

3

3

2

3

6

8

6

8

4

6

8

7

4

4

4

8

4

8

7
8 6

7
4

Blank, ½"Thick – Wood, Mahogany or Cedar

Plate 6. Horses' heads

26

HORSES' HEADS

The horses' heads shown in Figure 35 and Plate 6 are carved of cedar and fastened to a poplar background. This makes a good color combination, since the green-colored poplar contrasts well with the red-and-cream-striped cedar. If preferred, the horses' heads may be carved of mahogany.

There is considerable modeling on the horses' heads, and as a result they are a bit more difficult to carve than the plaques previously discussed.

First cut the outlines separating the head of the near horse from that of the other one. Then outline their tongues with two V cuts. Form the lips and tongue. Then outline the nostrils, just inside their bordering ridges and hollow them out to the proper depth. Outline the eyes and round over the eyeballs. Hollow the ears. Next round all edges. Complete the carving by carefully gouging out the low places and rounding the high places to form the valleys and ridges which make up the contours shown in Figure 35.

Fig. 35. Horses' heads

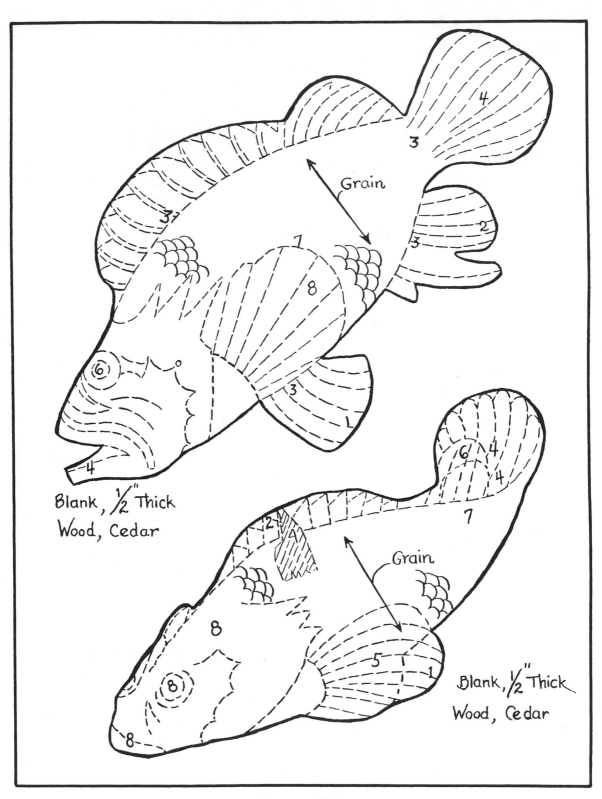

Grain

Blank, ½" Thick
Wood, Cedar

Grain

Blank, ½" Thick
Wood, Cedar

Plate 7. Goldfish

GOLDFISH

The frontispiece illustrates the beauty of the goldfish plaque, Figure 36 and Plate 7. Aromatic cedar, if carefully selected for color, with intermingled red and white streaks, makes an attractive plaque.

To carve the fish, outline the gills and fins. Trim the fins quite thin at the edges and notch the dividing lines. Outline and then carve the mouth and eye. The mouth of a fish has a riblike ridge which should be carefully rounded to get the proper effect. The eye has a ball-shaped pupil, partly covered with a thick membrane which shows in the carving.

After shaping the bony head structure, round the body, and then carefully indicate scales by making deep indentations with a narrow fluting tool or with a veiner.

Paint the background, wax and then fasten the fish to it.

Fig. 36. Goldfish

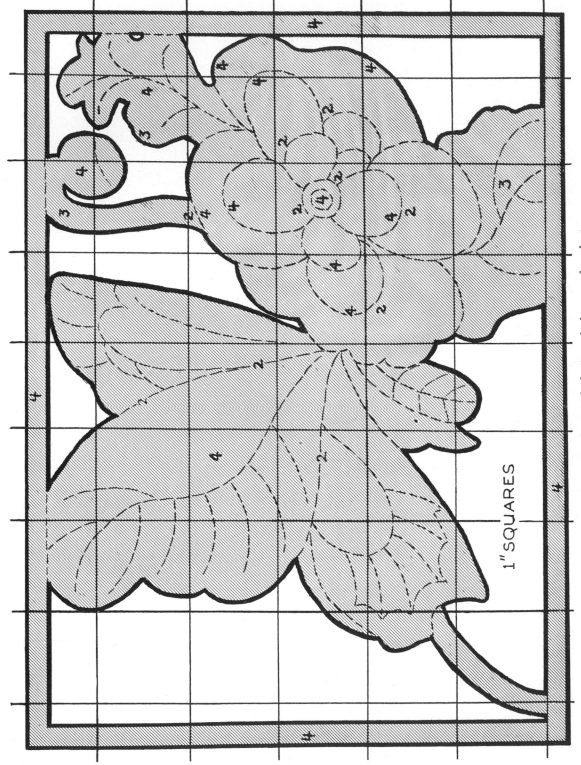

1" SQUARES

Plate 8. Butterfly plaque. Blank, ¾ in. thick — wood, walnut

30

Before beginning to carve the butterfly plaque, Figure 37 and Plate 8, jig-saw the background. Then outline each leaf and petal with deep V cuts. Round over the wings with a knife or a skew chisel. Carefully gouge out each petal. To complete the plaque, use a veiner to cut the fine lines shown in Figure 37.

Fig. 37. Butterfly plaque

1"SQUARES

Plate 9. Dogwood plaque. Blank, ½ in. thick — wood, poplar

32

Dogwood blossoms, shown in Figure 38 and Plate 9, are a symbol of springtime. The blossoms are very decorative and are not difficult to carve, since their outline is quite regular.

After cutting out the blank from a piece of poplar, first outline each blossom and every individual petal, leaf, and branch with a fine veining tool. This tool is better adapted to this particular job than a V tool, since too deep a cut is not likely to be made, and the rounded outline permits later trimming with other tools. This trimming follows after the background has been completely carved.

When finishing the background, be very careful to always cut in the same general direction. With a shallow gouge smooth-cut as you go, so that very little sanding will be required.

Round over each leaf and branch, and shape each petal. Outline each individual petal carefully and round it slightly. Cut shallow grooves on every petal with a veiner. Use a V tool on the center of each leaf.

Outline the border ornament, lower the background, and the carving is completed.

Fig. 38. Dogwood blossoms

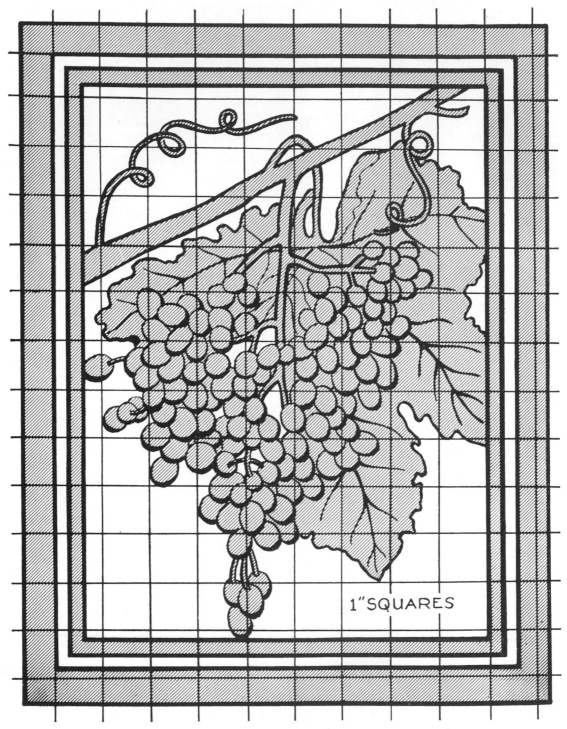

1"SQUARES

Plate 10. Grape plaque. Blank ½ in. thick — wood, poplar

34

CLUSTER OF GRAPES

If the dogwood plaque symbolizes spring, then the grape plaque, Figure 39 and Plate 10, may be said to symbolize fall. There is an opportunity to do a great deal of modeling on this poplar plaque, because the cluster of grapes, the leaf, and even the vine are wonderfully formed.

Every individual grape is carefully outlined and rounded. The effects of depth and perspective are achieved by partly submerging some of the grapes in the cluster. The leaf is deeply modeled, and then incised with deep V cuts. The twisted tendrils add interest and detail. The smooth texture of the fruit, leaf, and vine, throws them into bold relief against the rough-textured background.

Fig. 39. Cluster of grapes

CHAPTER 4

TRAYS AND BOOK ENDS

SERVING TRAYS

THE small serving trays, shown in Figure 43, are excellent for serving little snacks to guests. They are made of walnut with white pine ends. The outsides of the trays measure 17 in. long by 6½ in. wide by 1⅛ in. deep, as shown in Plate 14. The sides are ¼ in. thick, the bottom ⅜ in. thick, and the white pine ends ¾ in. thick.

Plate 13. Decorative carvings for serving trays

Fig. 43. Serving trays and other carvings

After the tray has been built, and before it is carved, Plate 13, cuts with a dado head are made under the white pine ends to form effective handles, Plate 14.

First outline the pattern and then trim away the wood. When completed, the trays are waxed.

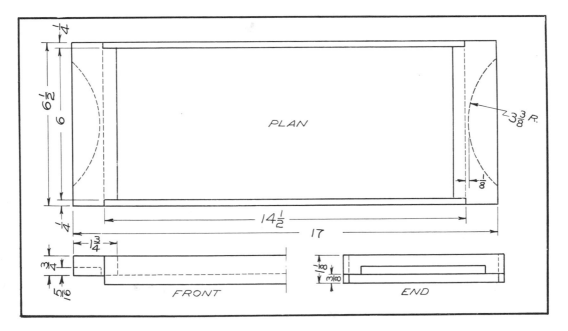

Plate 14. Plan for building trays

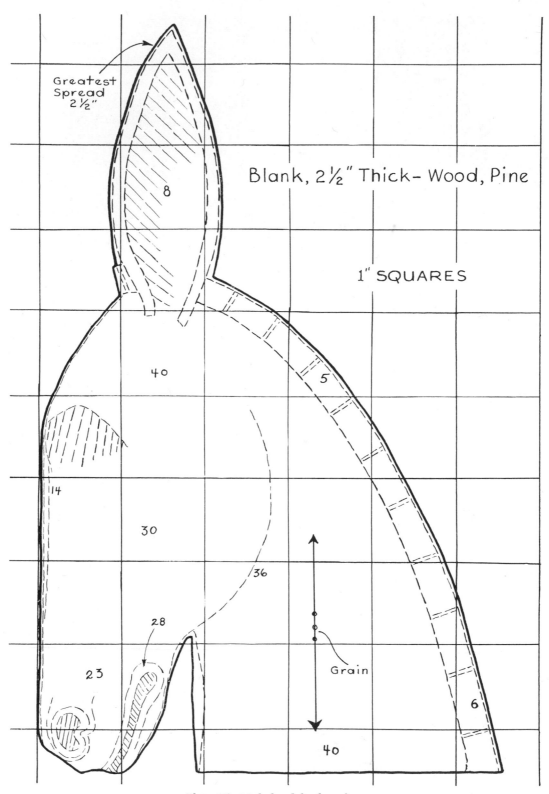

Greatest
Spread
2½"

8

Blank, 2½" Thick – Wood, Pine

1" SQUARES

40

5

14

30

36

Grain

28

23

6

40

Plate 15. Mule-head book ends

Book ends are always useful, but these carved ones are also distinctive.

The mule-head book ends are carved of white pine. Front and side views of both the blank and the completed heads are shown in Figure 44. As shown on Plate 15, the thickness of the blank is 2½ in.

First draw a center line down the front and down the back of the head. Then draw the jaw line, and also the lines down the back of the neck separating it from the mane.

Start carving by rounding the neck, Figure 44. Form the mane by trimming away the wood on each side of it to a depth of about ⅜ in.

To carve the head, first trim away under the eyes. No eyeballs or eye sockets are carved on this particular figure, these being left just as simple as it is possible to make them. The mouth and nostrils are more realistically formed, the treatment given them being in marked contrast to the treatment of the eyes.

Next, separate the ears by sawing out the unwanted stock with a coping saw, Figure 44. Trim the outsides of the ears first, then hollow them deeply on the opposite sides.

Cut the notches on the mane, sandpaper the figure, and it will be completed.

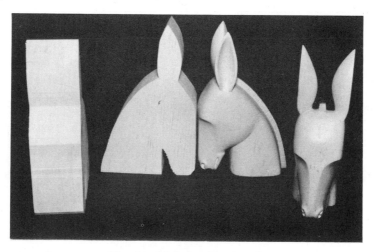

Fig. 44. Mule-head book ends

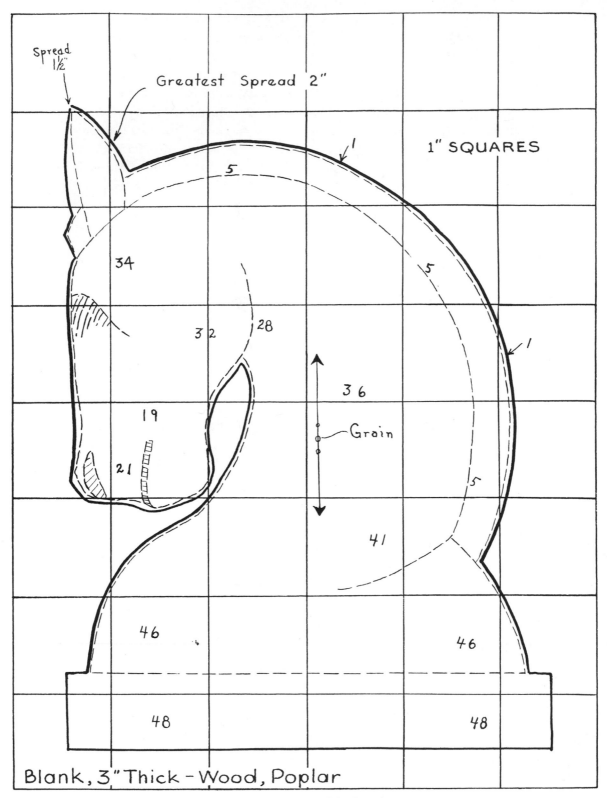

Plate 16. Horse-head book ends

Directions for carving the horse-head book ends would be so nearly like those for carving the mule-head book ends, that a separate, detailed description will be unnecessary. The book ends shown in Figure 45 and Plate 16 are carved of poplar, and are smooth-surfaced like the mule heads. In Figure 43 is shown a pair which has been treated in a more rugged manner.

The entire surface has been given an interesting texture by shallow, but carefully executed cuts with an extra flat.

Both of these book ends must be weighted with lead. In the middle of the bottoms, cut out a hole 1¼ by 1½ by 2 in. Melt lead and, with a ladle, pour it into the hole until it is filled. When this has hardened and cooled, glue a piece of felt to the base.

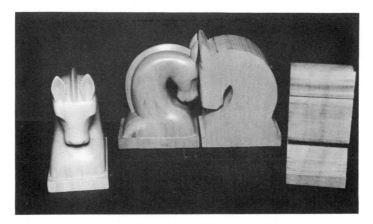

Fig. 45. Horse-head book ends

CHAPTER 5

JEWELRY

THOUGH most jewelry is fashioned from so-called precious materials, there is no reason why we should limit ourselves to these when making jewelry for ourselves. All jewelry should be a very personal item among anyone's possessions, and should, therefore, be unique as well as attractive. For these reasons it is highly desirable to have jewelry which is different from that which our friends may own. If this thesis strikes a favorable response on the reader's part, then what could be better than a piece of jewelry made of wood?

If the reader can carve something for himself, so much the better; and if he can design it also, that will be better still, for then indeed he should achieve distinction.

The designs shown in Figure 49 and Plate 19 should prove suggestive to those who are satisfied to merely reproduce the designs of others, as well as to those who plan to do original things of their own choosing.

Favorite hobbies and pets are always good for an idea for an original design. Later on many other ideas will suggest themselves to the reader.

To anyone who likes whittling, and has an odd moment of spare time only occasionally, these small unique pieces of craftsmanship will be ideally suited in enabling them to spend odd spare moments profitably. Jewelry findings, such as pins used to fasten them, may readily be bought by mail. They are inexpensive and are easily screwed to the backs of the pieces, Figure 48.

Fig. 48. Fastening pin screwed on the back of a piece of jewelry

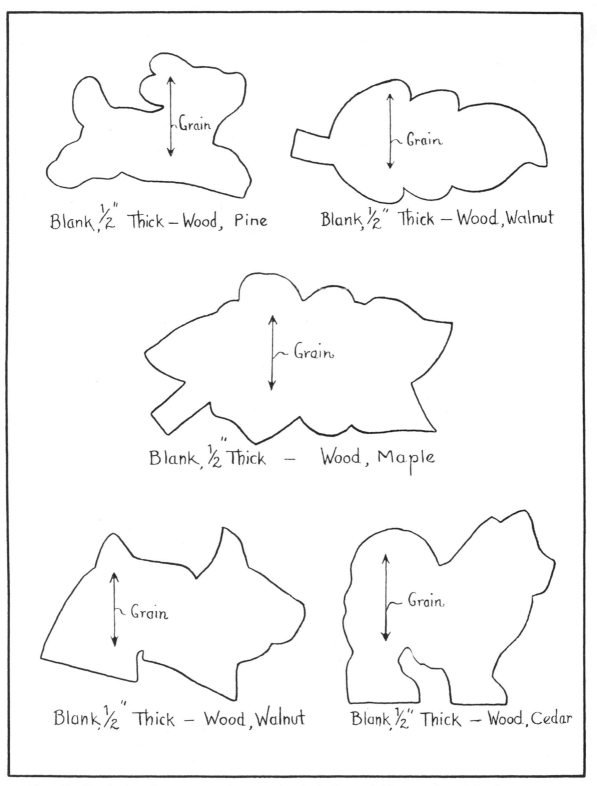

Blank, ½" Thick — Wood, Pine

Blank, ½" Thick — Wood, Walnut

Blank, ½" Thick — Wood, Maple

Blank, ½" Thick — Wood, Walnut

Blank, ½" Thick — Wood, Cedar

Plate 19. Wooden jewelry. Running dog, acanthus leaf, dogwood blossoms, horses' heads, and spitz

Fig. 49. Carved wooden jewelry. A, Horses' heads; B, small running dog; C, pin; D, spitz; E, dogwood blossom and leaves; F, acanthus leaf

HORSES' HEADS

To carve the horses' heads shown at *A*, in Figure 49, first cut a very shallow outline along the back of the neck of the lead horse. Outline the bridles, and round the necks and heads. Lower the background under the necklines, then cut the notches to form mouths and manes, thus completing the job.

SMALL RUNNING DOG

The small running dog shown at *B*, in Figure 49, is easily carved, since all that needs to be done is to round over the edges of the blank, and then cut the small facets which give this particular piece its rough appearance.

SPITZ

To carve the little spitz shown at *D*, in Figure 49, first round the body, thinning the blank on every edge, except at the bottoms of the feet, and the top of the head where the ears are to be. Next, cut the neckline and outline the fronts of the legs nearest to you. Cut the notch which separates the two hind legs, then round and shape them.

Shape the forelegs. Outline the tail where it is joined to the body by rounding the body to enable you to shape it properly.

Carve the head by first cutting a V groove for his mouth. Cut a notch under his forehead, thus making a place to carve his eyes. This notch should be perpendicular to the notch already cut to form his mouth. Trim his nose and forehead, thus partly forming his ears. Shape these as carefully as possible and then cut his eyes. The V-shaped grooves around the outline of his body will complete the job.

This carving is finished in dark red-brown water color and then waxed.

DOGWOOD BLOSSOM AND LEAVES

To carve the dogwood blossom shown at *E*, Figure 49, first outline each petal and leaf with sharp but shallow V cuts. Notice that each petal has a slightly rounded ridge in the center, while on each side of this ridge the petal is gouged out.

ACANTHUS LEAF

Leaves are often very simple to carve, and the one shown at *F*, Figure 49, is no exception. After trimming the blank to get the proper outline, make a narrow V cut along both sides of the stem from one end of the leaf to the other. Trim the stem to round it. Curve the surface of the leaf as shown in Figure 49, leaving the edges only about ⅛ in. thick. Then cut the short V-shaped veins. Notch the edges, and the leaf is carved.

CHAPTER 6

FIGURE CARVING

IN THIS chapter we shall consider carving in the round, or figure carving as it is sometimes called. Figure carving offers a great many more interesting possibilities than carving in low relief, or on a flat background, since the figures are three dimensional. On the whole it is also more difficult than most low-relief or flat-background carving.

Carving some animals, such as the pig for example, is comparatively simple since what facial expression there is, is easily delineated. Other difficult details encountered when carving human figures, such as habits of dress, need not be taken into consideration. For those just beginning to carve in the round, familiar domestic animals and pets, such as dogs, cats, etc., will make ideal subjects.

At the end of this chapter is "Scotty," a little dog considerably more difficult to carve than the other animals which come under consideration. Unlike the other animals, Scotty has a great deal of facial expression. Carving him will make the transition from animal to human forms easier, which is one reason he has been included at that place.

THE GOOSE

The goose, shown in Figure 52 and Plate 22, is the simplest figure on which

to begin carving.

The goose is carved of white pine.

To begin this carving, first draw a center line along the back of the blank from which the goose is to be carved. This line will extend from its bill to the tip of its tail. Then extend the center line down its breast and on the back of its tail. These center lines will help to keep the figure symmetrical.

With a broad-bladed knife, begin trimming away the surplus wood on the tail, cutting first on one side, then on the other. Do not attempt to round the tail at this time, but be satisfied to trim it to the proper thicknesses as indicated by the

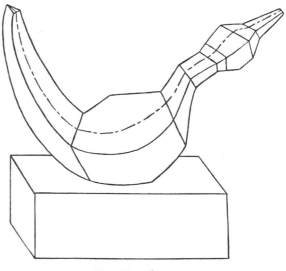

Fig. 52. The goose

46

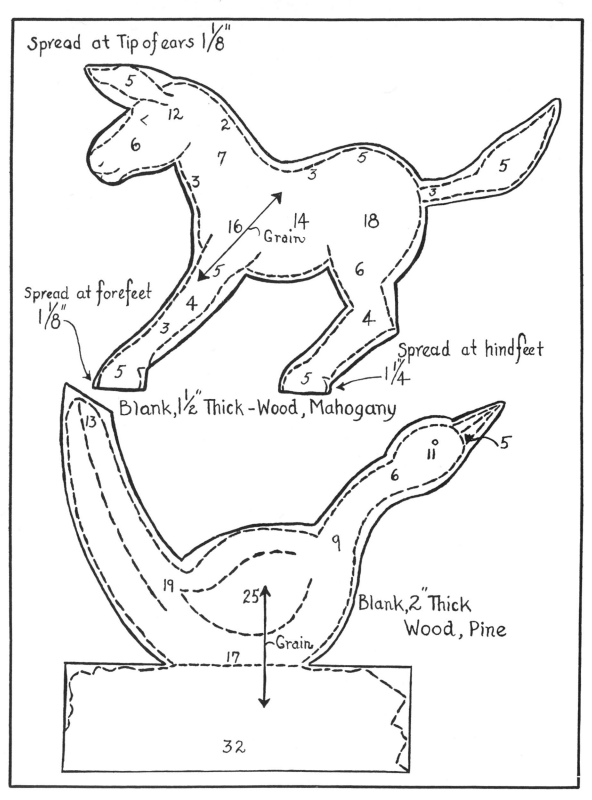

Plate 22. Mule and goose

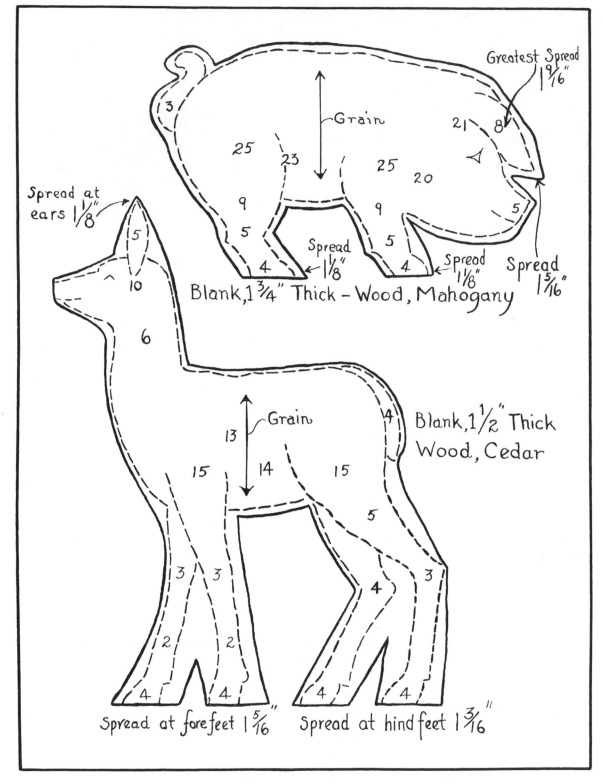

Plate 23. Pig and fawn

numbers on the drawing in Plate 22. Next, do the same thing on the body, leaving the neck and head until last, since they are thinner and more easily broken. If chisels are used, do this part of the work with a No. 5 or No. 6 gouge, cutting almost, or altogether, parallel with the grain. Be careful not to cut too deep, causing too great a piece to be split off.

In all forming operations, such as this, it will be easier to keep the parts roughly square or rectangular in section, until the desired thicknesses have been obtained throughout, see Figure 52. The figure will be more nearly symmetrical if this is done, since it is much simpler to measure or compare distances on each side of the center line than if the figure is rounded at once. By doing it this way, there is not nearly so much danger of cutting away more stock than is intended.

Once proper thicknesses on the tail, body, and neck have been arrived at, the boasting-in may begin on the figure to get the rough contour, shown at B, in Figure 2. This rounding of edges and corners may be done with a smaller knife blade, Figure 11, or with a skew and extra flats if chisels are being used.

Round all parts as smoothly as possible with slicing cuts of the tool. Trim the di-viding line between the goose and its base. Outline the wing with a small, pointed blade, or an acute-angled V tool. Then carve the base itself.

Sandpaper the figure. Hollow out and glue in black-headed pins for the eyes, and the goose will have been completed.

THE PIG

The pig, shown in Plate 23 and Figure 53, is almost as easy to carve as the goose. After the blank has been cut, there is some hollowing out to be done first between the forelegs and between the hind legs. This constitutes an advanced step not encountered when carving the goose. As in the goose, keep the members roughly square in section until the legs have been cut to the proper thicknesses, as indicated by the numbers in Plate 23.

If a knife is used, do this hollowing by first cutting a small notch, as at A, in Figure 54. This notch may be gradually made deeper, as at B, and C, until it finally assumes the shape shown at D. If chisels are available, a fluting tool or a No. 11 deep gouge will be very useful in completing this operation.

Now, once more draw a center line on the back and the belly of the blank from the pig's nose to his tail. Draw the

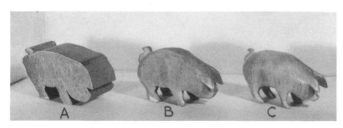

Fig. 53. The pig

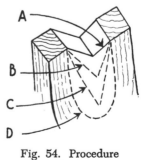

Fig. 54. Procedure for hollowing out

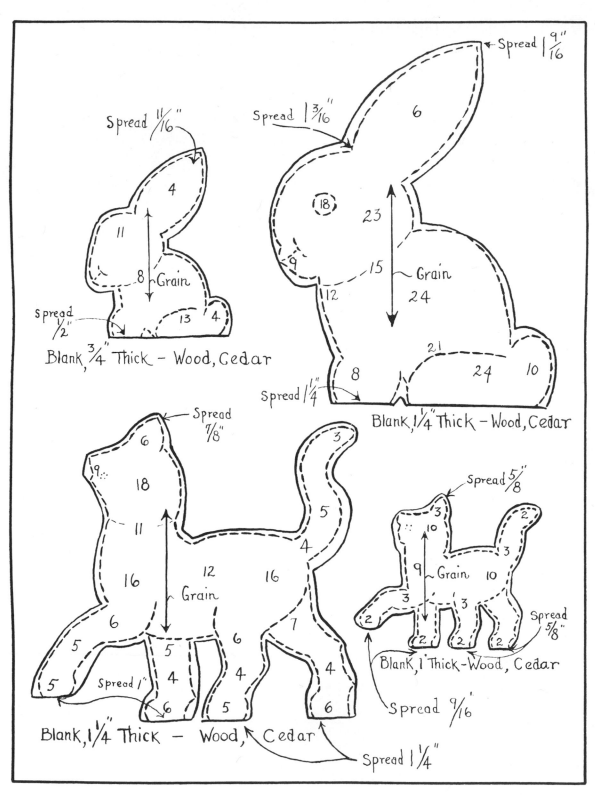

Plate 24. Rabbit family and cat family

line showing the thickness of the tail, which you may get from Plate 23. After having drawn lines indicating the outline of the rump, cut away excess stock to form the tail.

The pig's ears are spaced 9/16 in. apart at the point of their greatest spread. This distance is obtained by subtracting the sum of greatest thicknesses of the two ears from the greatest spread. Draw the outline of the ears, then carve between them. Cut away some of the wood just under the ears, thus pointing up his snout.

Now round his back, cutting first on one side, then shaping the opposite side to conform with the first. Shape the ears, rounding them on top like a drooped leaf. Put a cleft in his toes, remove triangular chips to make eyes, make two nostril holes, and carve two lines under his snout for his mouth, and the pig is finished.

THE RABBIT FAMILY

The rabbit family, as shown in Plate 24, is not difficult to carve. Other than separating the ears and rounding the bunny's back and face, there is very little carving to be done.

It is a good idea to begin with the ears. Separate them in the same manner as was described for the pig's hind feet. The spread of the ears is less at the head than at the tips, see Plate 24. In hollowing the ears, a No. 11 gouge will be very useful.

After the ears have been roughly shaped, as shown at B, Figure 55, outline the neckline, digging in with the point of the knife, or using a V tool. In the same manner, cut the curve made by his hind feet.

If it has not already been done, draw a center line down the middle of his back, and down his front as well. Cut away the excess wood to form his tail, partly rounding his back in so doing. Finish rounding his body and then round his head to resemble the shape of an egg. His front feet are divided by only a small notch, about ¼ in. deep.

His eyes may be carved as shown in Figure 55, but two white, roundheaded pins will give him a more realistic appearance, see Figure 56.

The small bunnies are carved in exactly the same way as the large ones.

THE ELEPHANT

If you recall your boyhood days at the circus with pleasure, you may want to carve an elephant. To have one with his trunk turned in is bad luck, they say; and though we are not superstitious about such matters, someone else may be, so we've turned this one's trunk out.

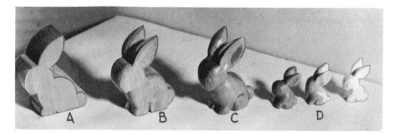

Fig. 55. The rabbit family

51

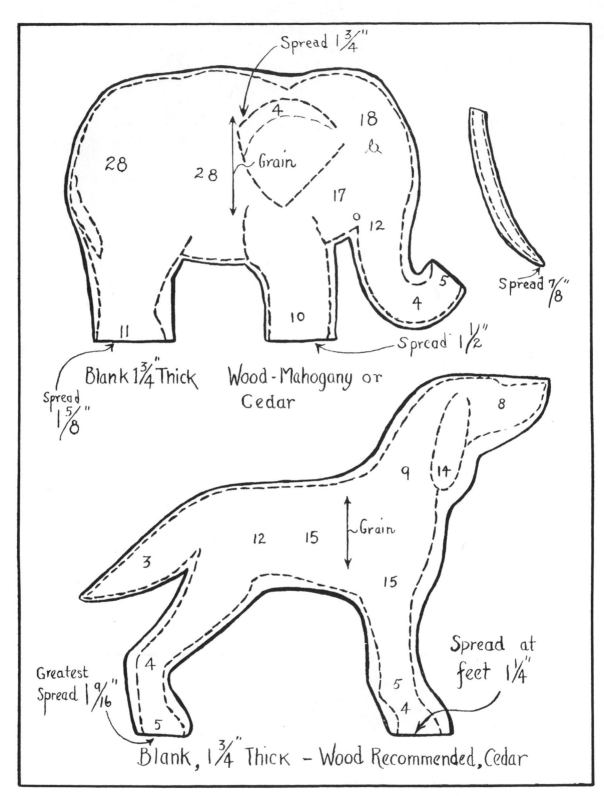

Plate 25. Elephant and bird dog

Fig. 56. Carved figures

Old Jumbo is not difficult to carve. His body has no more shape than a haystack with a rounded top and straight sides. Also his legs are straight, and, therefore, easily formed. His head is shaped like an Easter egg, and would look a great deal like one were it not for the dangling trunk and the wide, flaplike ears. He can be easily cut with a pocketknife, see Figure 57 and Plate 25.

To carve him, first draw the center line from the outside of his dangling trunk to his tail. Draw an egg-shaped oval on his forehead. Reduce the thickness sharply where the head joins the trunk. Under the offset thus formed, drill ⅛-in. holes for the tusks, which are carved of some white wood, such as white pine or maple. Leave his trunk square at first, until after it has been cut down to its proper thickness. Then round it and the head as well. Draw the ears, and outline them with the point of a knife or a V tool. They are undercut only a little bit along the top edges. The neckline under the ears could most easily be done with a fluting tool.

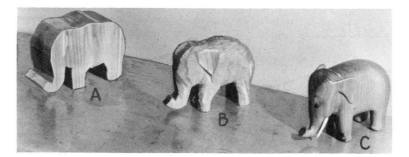

Fig. 57. The elephant

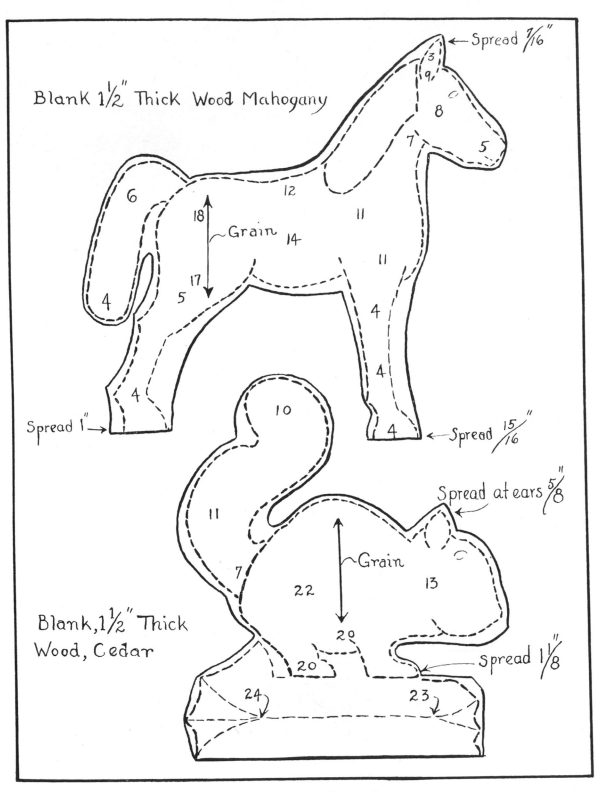

Plate 26. Horse and squirrel

Cut notches to start hollowing out between the legs, as was done in carving the pig. Leave the legs square until all the hollowing out has been done and until his belly has been rounded. Then round them off.

Complete him by tucking his tail on the inside of his right hind leg, see Plate 25. For eyes, drive two black-headed beaded pins into the wood.

THE SQUIRREL

The squirrel's head and body are turnip shaped, see Figure 58 and Plate 26. This one seems to be sitting on a rock.

First draw a center line from his nose to his tail.

Mark the thickness of the tail, and with a broad-bladed knife cut away the sides of the block to give the tail its proper thickness. Then begin rounding the back of the body and the head. The overlapping turnip-shaped outlines, Figure 59, on the side of the blank will give the neckline,

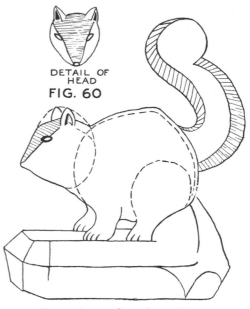

DETAIL OF HEAD
FIG. 60

Fig. 59. Rounding the neckline and back of the squirrel

which may be cut with a fluting tool, or with a knife if preferred.

The squirrel's ears are not much more than ¼ in. long, and the top of his head is nearly level with their tips, so notch out

Fig. 58. The squirrel

55

alongside of each ear to form the top of the head, as in Figure 60.

Finish rounding the head and body down to the legs. Cut deeply on both sides of the blank, thus separating the fore from the hind feet, and making it possible to round the under part of his body. In doing this, a spoon gouge will prove very useful. It will also be a good tool to employ when gouging out the wood between his fore-feet. The small blade of a knife will do very well to shape the feet. With a broad-bladed knife bevel and notch the side of the stone on which he is resting. Then round up and form his tail; cut his eyes, nose, and mouth with the end of a narrow blade, thus completing the job.

BIRD DOG

With the bird dog you will begin a more difficult subject than any that has so far been considered in this chapter. This is so because his head, legs, and body have more refinements of shape and form than the ones we have thus far described. Also, members, such as his legs, are more deli-

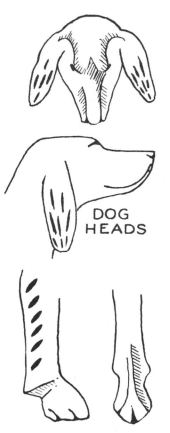

Fig. 62. Finishing details of the eyes, nostril holes, nose, and paws of the bird dog

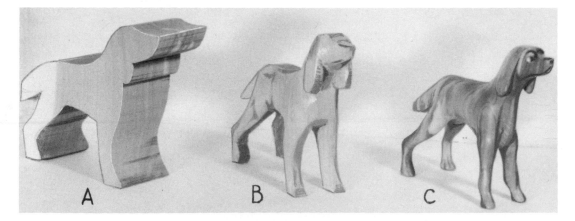

Fig. 61. The bird dog

cate in scale than the legs of the elephant, or even the pig, and therefore will require a great deal more care in cutting. This greater care is essential, not only to avoid breaking them, but because, if they are carelessly shaped or left with too much wood on them, they may resemble the legs of a cow more than they will a dog's. This is the case at the end of the boasting-in stage, shown at *B* in Figure 61. Consequently the final shaping of these members must be attended to most carefully to avoid poor proportions.

Draw the necessary center lines, as explained for former projects, since his body will be symmetrical.

There should be no difficulty in boasting-in this part of the carving. Determine the thicknesses of head, body, and tail, working always from the center line. Draw outlines for each side and trim away the excess wood alongside these members. Attempt no shaping as yet, until the proper maximum thicknesses of the above members has been obtained.

Now remove the excess thickness from each side of the legs, determining the amount from the spread indicated at the feet in Plate 25. Then cut away the unwanted wood between his hind legs and his forelegs, but at all times leave the members square in section. Not until each member has been trimmed to its approximate thickness, as shown in Plate 25, should contours be rounded. This precaution will make the final task easier, and will save much recutting and guesswork.

Trim between the ears, under his neck, and then shape his forehead. Round and shape his body next; then each leg,

leaving his tail until last, to lessen the danger of breaking it off.

Now begin to put in the more delicate details. First, carve his eyes, then his nostril holes and nose, see Figure 62. Carve his toes, and then put in a few fine V lines on his tail, ears, chest, and body, just in front of his back legs.

SMALL HORSES

Carving the small horse, Figure 63, Plate 26, is so nearly like carving the bird dog, that instructions for doing one could just as well apply to the other. His back legs are, perhaps, a trifle more difficult to do than the dog's, and his ears stick up above his head instead of hanging down. Otherwise the differences are so inconsequential that little additional instruction regarding this carving need be given.

The horse's mane is carved always on the right side of his neck.

At *A*, in Figure 9 is shown a horse which is carved a bit differently from the others. This horse, instead of being smoothed like the one at *B*, is carried only a little beyond the boasting-in stage. Occasionally, this treatment is very effective, but the final cutting must be more, rather than less carefully done, in order to get the right effect. This rough and angular technique gives the effect of having been done by rapid strokes of a small blade. This gives the vitality that is sometimes lost in too much detail cutting. Broad cuts of the knife produce effects of rhythm. A cut may begin on the top of the ears and be carried to the tip of the tail. The cuts are broken to keep the line interesting The stubborn donkey, made of mahogany,

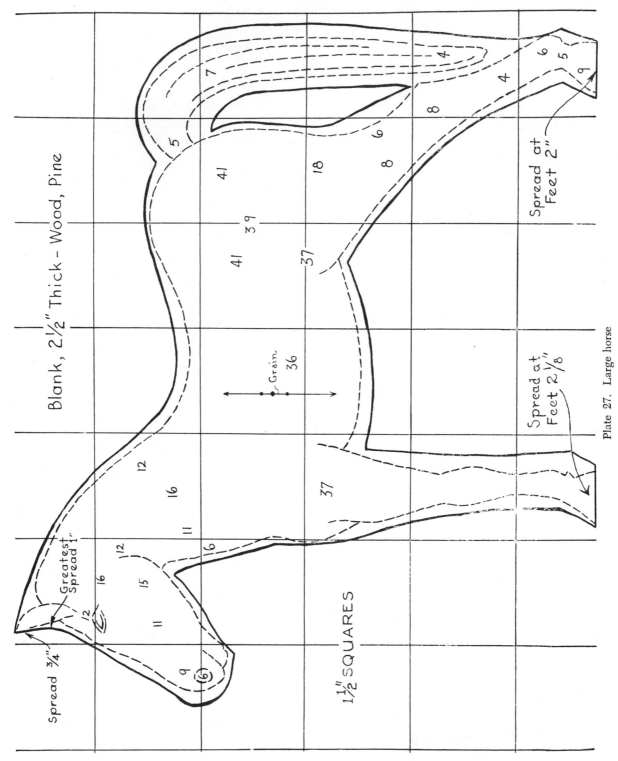

Blank, 2½" Thick – Wood, Pine

7

5

41

4

8

6

4

6

5

9

Spread at
Feet 2"

18

8

41 3 9

41

37

Grain
36

12

16

37

11

6

12 12

Greatest
Spread 1"

16

15

Spread ¾"

12

11

9
6

Spread at
Feet 2⅛"

1½" SQUARES

Plate 27. Large horse

Fig. 63. Small horse

is a good example of this technique. One of the hardwoods is best for this type of cutting because the cuts can be kept clean from ragged edges. No sanding is necessary.

LARGE HORSE

Some carvers may wish to try a larger horse than those we have just discussed.

On Plate 27 is a design for such a horse. The completed figure is shown at *C* in Figure 64. On this particular figure we undertake to show the muscles in the legs, and a little more detail at the eyes and nose, but otherwise the job will entail practically the same problems as carving the small horse.

Fig. 64. Large horse

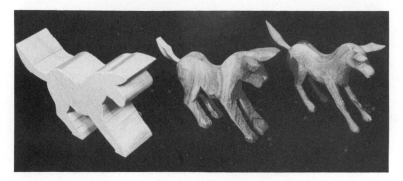

Fig. 65. The mule

MULE

If the reader has ever worked a mule, the one shown in Figure 65 and Plate 22 may bring back memories. But even if the reader's acquaintance with this recalcitrant breed of quadruped has been less intimate, he will probably get a "kick" out of carving him. If he wished, he might even give him an appropriate name such as, "Unwilling."

In carving him, Plate 22, care must be taken not to break off his tail, since it is rather thin where it connects with his body. The grain of the wood runs across the tail instead of paralleling it. If so desired, his tail may be carved separately, and the grain may be run the other way. A hole may be drilled, into which the tail may be glued. It is, however, a matter of pride with most wood carvers to be able to accomplish the job by using only a single piece of wood. Looking at Plate 22, it will be noticed that the grain of the wood should run parallel to the front legs. This gives the maximum amount of strength to the weakest members of this figure.

The ears of the mule are also rather easily broken. Once the job has been successfully accomplished, it is this additional care, necessary to successfully complete this figure, which will mark the carver as having advanced one more step in the art of wood carving.

FAWN

Advancing in the art of wood carving step by step, brings us next to the fawn in Figure 66 and Plate 23. This carving is one of the most appealing of any discussed in this chapter. What makes it different, and also more difficult to carve than the horse or dog, is the fact that the legs are not in line with each other as they are on the other figures. They are also very thin, though wonderfully well proportioned.

In carving the legs of this beautiful creature, first trim them on the outside, from the hips to the ground, to the thicknesses given in Plate 23. Keep the sides of the legs flat, as shown at B, Figure 66. Then part the right and left legs as was done on the other figures which have already been discussed. But, instead of keeping the eight feet which are thus formed,

60

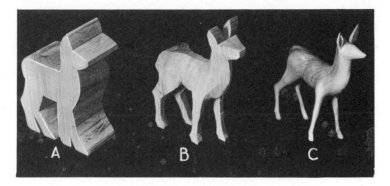

Fig. 66. The fawn

simply cut away the four which are not needed, from the knees down. The remaining operations are the same as for the horse or the dog, except that the faun's legs are so delicately proportioned that the greatest care must be exercised in order to do a good job.

THE CAT FAMILY

As in the case of the fawn, so the legs of the cat are not in line with each other. What makes it slightly more difficult than the faun is the fact that their bodies are in motion instead of at rest. The cats are apparently "taking the air," as shown in Figure 67 and Plate 24. Has there ever, we

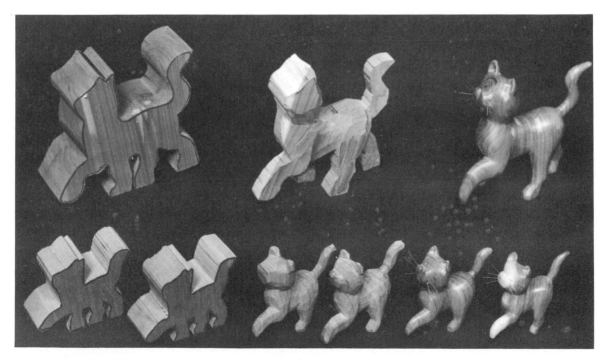

Fig. 67. The cat family

Fig. 68. Right view of Scotty

"Hoot mon!, and what be ye staring at?" "At the most appealing representation of dogdom I have ever seen," you might answer. And while Scotty is the most difficult to carve of all the animals shown, he is also the most appealing little figure of them all. Anyone who has a little dog like this of his own to love should love his little wooden counterpart just about as well once it has been carved.

What makes him somewhat more difficult to carve than the others, is the fact that nothing about him is symmetrical. From the sad, but knowing expression on his face, it may be surmised that he finds the world to be just about as much out of balance as he is.

There is very little that we can tell which will help in carving him, except to urge anyone who wishes to do so to try

wonder, been such a "stuck-up" family of cats as this one? Judging from the way they strut, they must indeed be of a royal line of cats. Possibly they are on their way to look at the king, or it is just barely possible they have already seen him!

Anyway it's a lot of fun to carve them, and a touch of originality of your own may possibly be added in the angle at which their snooty heads are cocked.

Their whiskers are made of toothbrush bristles, and the holes into which they are glued are made with pins.

Fig. 69. Left view of Scotty

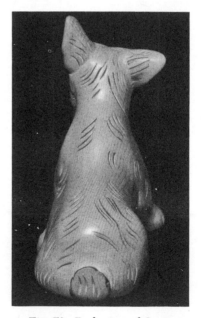

Fig. 70. Back view of Scotty

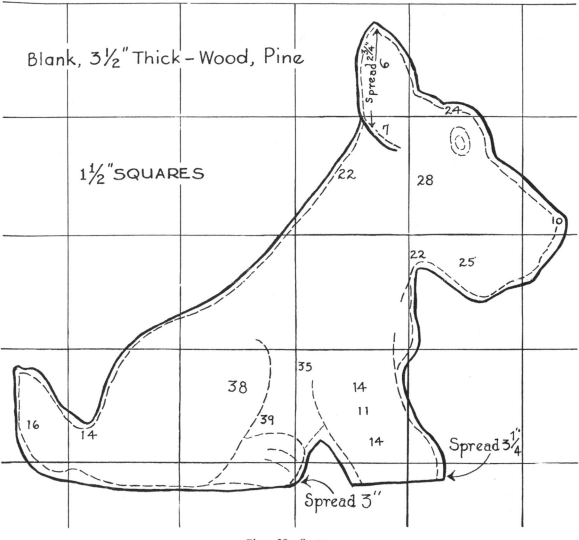

Blank, 3½" Thick – Wood, Pine

1½" SQUARES

Spread 2¾

6

7

24

22

28

10

22

25

35

38

14

11

39

16

14

14

Spread 3¼"

Spread 3"

Plate 28. Scotty

several of the other animals before attempting to carve Scotty. The thicknesses given on Plate 28 must be regarded mostly as helpful approximations, since Scotty's shape changes so rapidly from one point to the next. His right side, for example, does not have much slope, while his left side slopes a great deal, see Figures 68, 69, and 70. His right ear is almost parallel with the top of his head, while his left is cocked at a more rakish angle.

His face has a great deal of expression, which we have succeeded in bringing out in the photographs, in order that it may be duplicated faithfully. Once Scotty has been completed the carver will be ready to tackle the problems in the following chapter.

CHAPTER 7

HUMAN FIGURES

NEGRO PREACHER

IN FIGURE 73 are shown 3 stages in the carving of the negro preacher. After the blank has been cut out, first draw a center line all the way down his front and back. Parts of this line are shown very clearly at *B*, in Figure 73. Then draw the necklines on the sides of the blank and the lines separating the bottom of his coat from his trousers. On the right side draw

his partly closed hand, leaving the index finger to point upward at the same angle as the bible he is holding in his left hand, and directly in line with it. Then carefully draw lines to separate the right hand from the bible.

Now draw the right hand, after which the carving may begin. Start by making a deep V cut to separate his legs and feet,

Fig. 73. The negro preacher

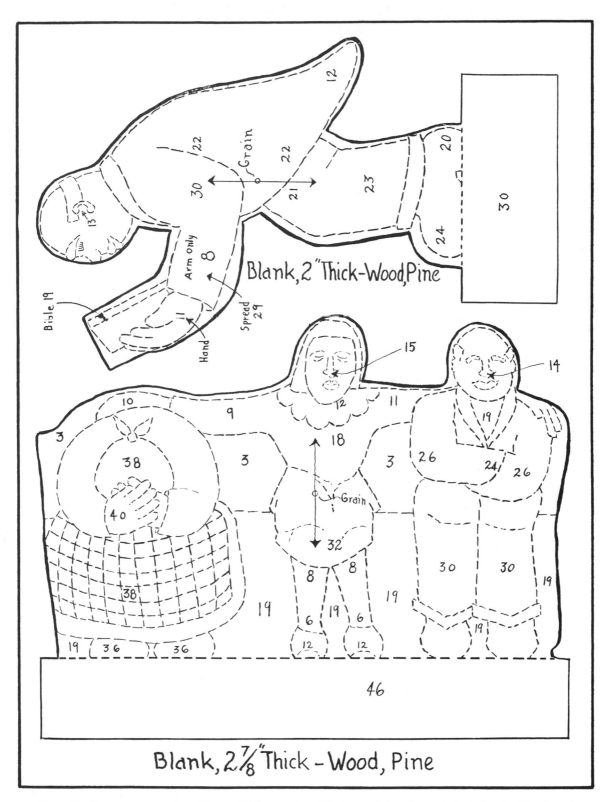

Plate 31. Negro congregation. Note: Thicknesses on girl's legs and feet do not include bench. All others do

Fig. 74. Carved figures

both in front and behind. When this is deep enough, start rounding over the legs as shown at *B*. All the thicknesses are given in Plate 31.

Before trimming away to form his head, draw lines for his elbows and sleeves. This will help to determine the amount of rounding which can be given to his shoulders and to the upper part of the sleeves, just back of the cuff on the right side.

Trim away the wood to get the proper thickness of his head. Then begin rounding it over as shown at *B*, Figure 73. Separate his right hand from the bible and begin rounding his shoulders and the back of his coat. The rough boasting-in is now completed and the finer details can be considered next.

Draw the cuffs on his trousers, then draw lines on top of his shoes in order to carve them. Keep rounding the legs, being as careful as possible to shape them as shown at *C* in Figure 73. Carve the cuffs of his trousers and complete his shoes. Trim the bottom of his coat and vest and round the bottoms of the arms.

Next, in completing the shaping of his back, don't forget to carve the buttons as shown in Figure 74.

Round the back of his head sufficiently to draw the ring of hair, and his ears. These should then be carved.

The most difficult parts to be carved next will be his face and his hands; his face being, perhaps, the easier of the two. Carefully draw his nose, eyes, mouth, and chin. Cut triangular-shaped notches, *A*, Figure 75, to form the nose and eyebrows, and in these notches, later on, carve the eyes. Then carve his mouth as shown in *B*, Figure 75. Give him beetling eyebrows by trimming away some of the wood above

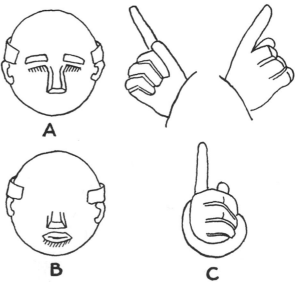

Fig. 75. Details of the preacher's head and hand

Fig. 76. The congregation

them. Form his chin, and the face will have been completed.

Next, draw the fingers on his right hand and also draw the thumb which closes over the top of his middle finger, see Figure 75. Make V cuts to separate the fingers, round them over as carefully as possible, and the job will be completed, see Figure 76.

CONGREGATION

The congregation, Figures 76 and 77, and Plate 31, is a companion piece to the negro preacher. The most difficult part of doing this carving is the deep undercutting which it entails. Much of this excess wood may be drilled out, but care must be taken not to drill too close to the parts you wish to keep.

It is always best to block out figures such as this, in square or rectangular sections if possible, getting each individual element to its proper thickness, width, and length before attempting to do any round-

ing over. This is an aid toward getting the right proportions and makes the final cutting much easier, see Figure 77.

As much as possible of the bench and floor, between each figure and at each end, should be done first. This will help in forming the figures and in getting them properly placed.

The first figure to carve is the girl in the center. First, a great deal of hollowing out will have to be done in back, and between the legs of this figure. Then trim her legs and feet. These need very little forming except to round them. Her dress is also very simple, and especially so, if the thicknesses have been properly blocked out beforehand. Round all parts of her body, leaving her collar raised about 1/16 in. Her face and her father's also are quite simple to carve. Cut deep V-shaped notches under her forehead and on each side of her nose to form her eyes, see *A*, Figure 77. To form the rest of her face is merely a rounding-over process.

67

Fig. 77. Detailed views of the congregation

To carve the girl's mother, cut away around the bottom of her skirt to form her shoes, which look much like two oblong black cough drops. Her checkered apron is raised about 1/16 in. above her dress.

With a V tool, cut deeply around her waist and under her arms in front. Then trim away the upper part of the apron, and round the bottoms of the arms. Next cut two deep, V-shaped notches on each side of her head to form the crooks of her arms. Outline her hands and the knot of the kerchief on her head. Round her back, and in so doing finish the details on the girl's right hand.

To carve her father, cut a deep V cut to separate his two legs. Trim out between his feet. Form the cuffs on his trousers and round over the tops and sides of his shoes. Make V cuts along the bottom of his coat and under his arms, cutting a deep notch at the center, where his folded arms rest on his lap. Cut a shallow V groove to sep-

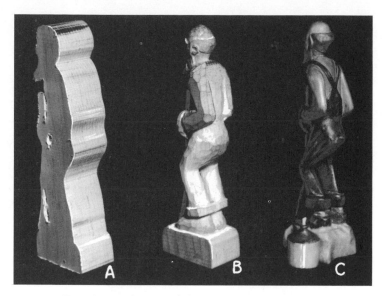

Fig. 78. Back view of the mountaineer moonshiner

arate the tops of his arms from his coat. Carve his tie. Draw his hair, his ears, and other face details; then carve them.

Each figure is rather deeply undercut in the back where it rests against the back of the bench.

When all sanding has been done, the figures may be painted and waxed.

MOUNTAINEER MOONSHINER

This old codger is not very difficult to carve, for even the lines of his face are

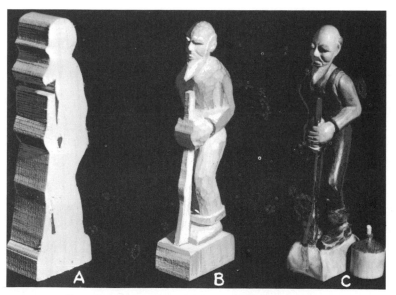

Fig. 79. Front view of the mountaineer moonshiner

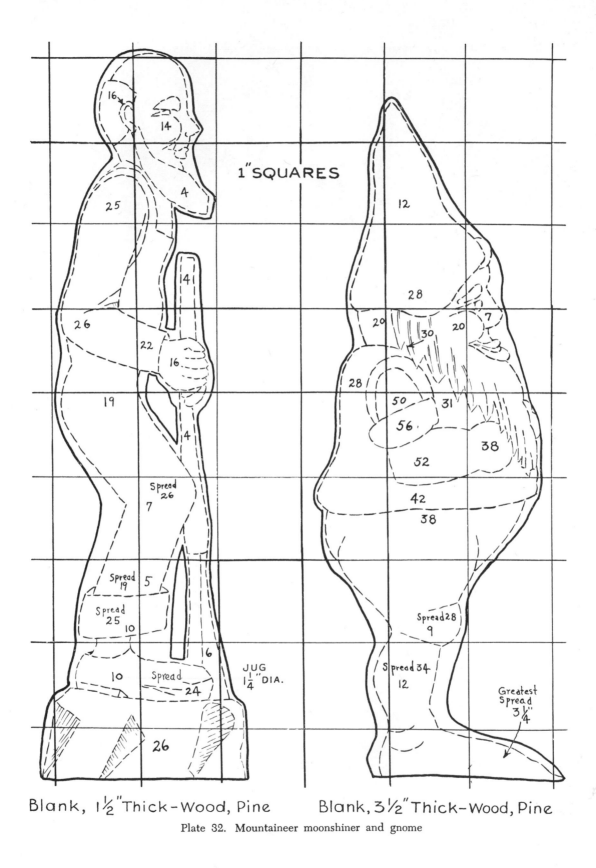

1" SQUARES

Blank, 1½" Thick – Wood, Pine   Blank, 3½" Thick – Wood, Pine

Plate 32. Mountaineer moonshiner and gnome

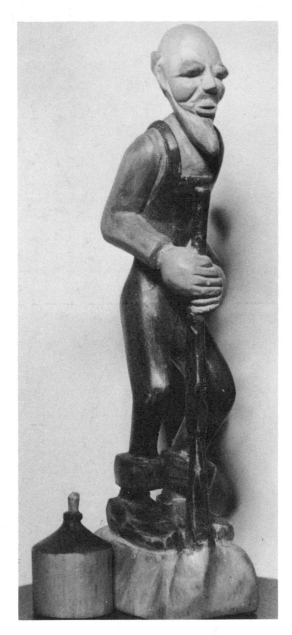

Fig. 80. Mountaineer moonshiner

Some drilling is necessary on this blank, to separate the gun from the body, thus making it easier for the knife to reach these places. The blank may also be drilled in back to separate the legs and feet.

First, draw vertical center lines on the front and back. These will help to locate the position of the gun, and other details as well. Then draw the profile on the back of the blank. The jug is carved separately and then glued to the figure after it has been completed.

Notch in and cut away under his arms. Draw the cuffs on the bottom of his overalls, and trim his legs. Round the lower parts of his body, and then draw his galluses and carve them. Notch in the neckline, and notch in a line above the hair of his head. Round the dome of his head, then trim the back of his feet, and the base.

Going to the front of the figure now, Figure 80, start trimming away on each side of the gun until it stands free, and until all body thicknesses have been obtained. Boast-in the body until it looks like *B* in Figure 79. Draw his overall shoulder straps and carve. Notch in deeply under his eyes and alongside his nose. Then trim his beard. Complete the figure by carving all the finer details, such as eyes, mouth, and fingers.

GNOME

This little gnome might be one of Santa Claus's assistants, from the looks of him. He's a pert little fellow. If he is to be left unpainted, he may be carved of cedar; otherwise white pine will be best, as shown in Figure 83.

quite simply and crudely formed. This is purposely done to emphasize the hillbilly effect so graphically illustrated in the photograph.

71

Fig. 81. The gnome

To carve him, Figures 81 and 82, first draw vertical center lines on the front and back of the blank. The excess stock between his legs may be sawed out, but leave enough to allow for trimming.

Draw the profiles, showing his shapes as viewed from the front and back (Figures 83 and 84), and boast-in the sides of the figure to this outline.

Since the profiles of the back and front have already been cut on the band saw, start carving his back, this being the easiest part. Draw lines for his neck, waist, bottom of his coat, seat of his pants, and

hollow of his legs at back and ankles. Then draw the backs of his arms and the rolled-up cuffs of his shirt. By following the photographs, Figures 82 and 84, there should be no difficulty in completing the carving of his back.

To carve the front of the lower part of his body is just as simple. Keep working upward, leaving his hands and face until last. Both the drawing, Plate 32, and Figure 83, clearly show the lines which should be drawn to begin carving the face and hands. Notch deeply under and at the sides of his nose, and also under his eye-

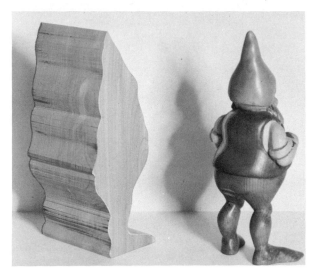

Fig. 82. Back view of the gnome

Fig. 83. Details of face

Fig. 84. Back profile

brows. His eyes protrude, so leave enough stock to carve them. Hollow out a groove above his beard with a fluting tool. With a V tool and a veiner, form the threadlike folds of his beard. After forming his fingers, the finishing touches, such as his eyebrows, eyeballs, distended nostrils, and protruding lips, should be carefully completed.

73

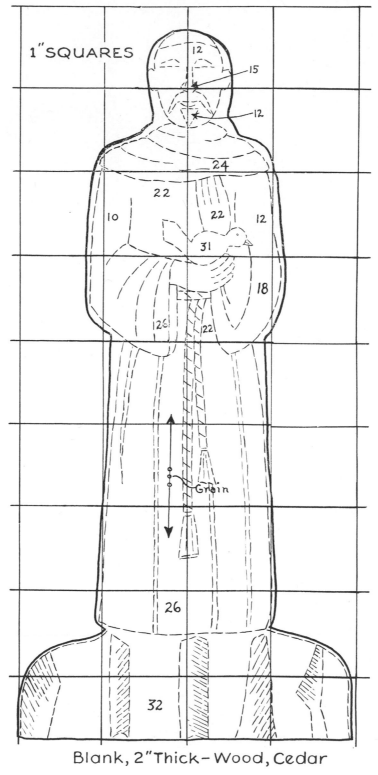

Blank, 2"Thick—Wood, Cedar

Plate 33. St. Francis

Fig. 85. St. Francis

ST. FRANCIS

The figure of St. Francis, Figures 85 and 86, and Plate 33, is carved of cedar. If a piece, having quite a few white streaks, is selected, the figure will take on added beauty. This is especially true if the streaks appear in the folds of the garment. Creamy sap streaks, intermingled with red, in these places, will be strikingly handsome.

The bottom of the figure is not difficult to carve, for the robe falls clear to the floor.

Draw the tasseled girdle, where it hangs down in front of the robe. In back, draw the top of the robe where it forms a cape over his shoulder. Make V cuts to outline his arms, and cut the figure in back as shown at *B*, in Figure 86. The bird on his shoulder and the one in his hands may be carved separately. These may then be fastened to his hand and shoulder with small wooden pegs and glue. Complete the cape in front. Draw and boast-in his sleeves and his hands. Make V cuts for the folds and fingers, and complete this part of the figure.

Fig. 86. Back view of St. Francis

To form his face, Figure 85, notch in on each side of his nose and under his eyebrows. Draw the ears, and trim around them at the same time as the eyes, nose, and mouth are being formed.

When the figure has been completed, carve the two birds, and drill holes large enough for tiny dowels formed of matchsticks, to be inserted. With these used as pegs, glue the birds to his hands and shoulder.

Carve the base, sand, and the figure is completed.

Dan'l Boone in coonskin cap is carved of cedar, Figure 88.

The blank should be drilled under his right arm to make cutting through easier, Figure 89.

Note that his gun is carved from the front part of the blank, while Dan'l himself is carved from the back of the blank. Thus this fact should be noted in drawing the profile on the sides of the blank.

Begin by drawing vertical lines to get the over-all thickness of his body, and then the gun. Trim away the unwanted wood.

76

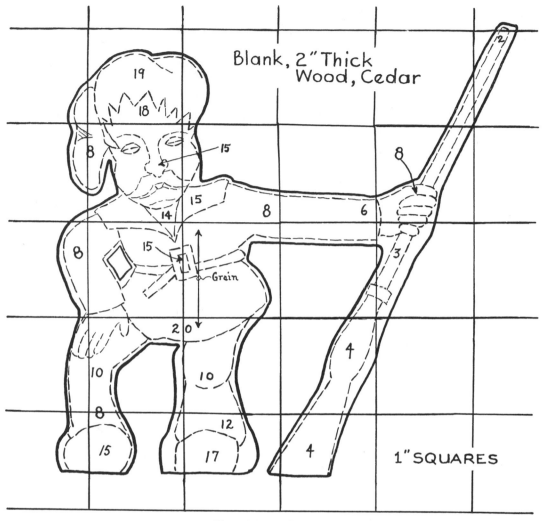

Blank, 2" Thick
Wood, Cedar

1" SQUARES

Plate 34. Dan'l Boone

Then on his back and front, draw the neck, waist, bottom of coat, and ankle lines. On the sides, draw his arms, the dangling tail of his coonskin cap, and the curves showing his bent knees.

Now begin carving his back, first notching out around his waist where his belt is to go; then around the back of his neck, and under his coat. Roughly trim the back of his head, as shown at B, in Figure 90. Trim his waist, and round his shoulders, his arms, the bottom of his coat, and the backs of his legs.

Go now to the front of the figure and round his waist, and at the same time rough-in the belt, as shown at B, in Figure 89. Notch in under his chin, and roughly round his face and head. Draw his right hand, if this has not already been done; then carve it, and roughly round his legs and feet.

It is a good idea to complete the carv-

77

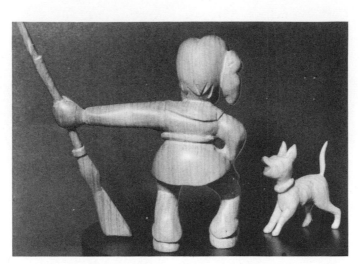

Fig. 87. Back view of Dan'l Boone

Fig. 88. Dan'l Boone

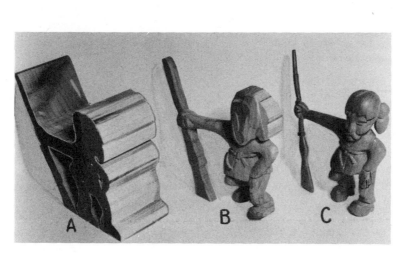

Fig. 89. Three stages of carving the figure of Dan'l Boone

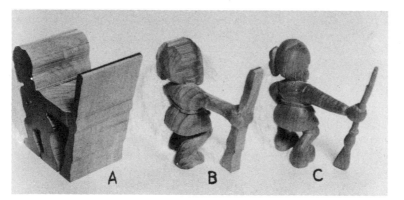

Fig. 90. Back view of Dan'l Boone

ing of his body before beginning on his face. Besides putting in the collar lines, fingers, belt buckle, and the line where his coat overlaps in front, little needs to be done except to smooth and round what has already been boasted-in.

Draw the outline of his coonskin cap, and notch out under it. Smooth the face sufficiently so the details may be drawn in. Then draw a vertical center line to help in placing his nose. Draw lines for his eyebrows, his one ear, the bottoms of his drooped eyelids, under his cheeks where they are separated from his mustache, under his mustache, and at the sides of his nose, see Figures 88, 91, and 92.

The details, shown in B, Figure 89, are now ready to be carved and should occasion very little difficulty if a close examination is made of how they have been done.

Dan'l's left arm and the gun have been saved until last, because they are the most delicate parts and the most easily broken. The actual carving of these members is not difficult, except possibly the hand clasping the gun barrel. To carve

Fig. 91. Side view of Dan'l Boone

the hand, first trim the wrist, and roughly round the hand. Draw and then carve in fingers and thumb. Whatever needs to be done to the gun will be self-evident if the photographs are examined.

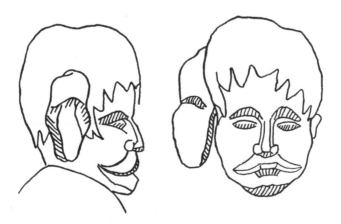

Fig. 92. Details for face of Dan'l Boone

80

CHAPTER 8

FINISHING

AFTER the figures have been carved, their beauty and value is greatly enhanced by the proper kind of finish. In this chapter we will take up the proper methods of finishing, which differ in a great many respects from the methods and finishes used on other kinds of woodwork.

Number 4/0 garnet paper is about the roughest that should be used to sandpaper the carvings. This should be followed by No. 6/0 garnet paper. Garnet paper is red in color, and the grits are a great deal sharper and harder than those found on white flint papers. Then garnet paper costs a little more than flint paper, but the quicker, more efficient job it does, more than compensates for the added cost. Number 6/0 paper has a thin backing, and is ideally suited for getting into difficult corners and inaccessible grooves.

Figure 27 shows the proper way of holding the sandpaper. A full-sized sheet of garnet paper is cut or torn into eight equal parts. Each of these parts will be large enough, when rolled to form a hollow cylinder, to be held loosely in the hand while sanding, as shown in Figure 27. Real fine details, such as eyes, or very sharp lines, must be more carefully sanded. The sharp edge of a newly cut piece of sandpaper must be very lightly and carefully rubbed along the sides forming such sharp edges, so as not to destroy their sharpness. Frequent rubbings, rather than hard pressure, should be relied upon to smooth such delicate details.

It has been said that it takes as long to sand a carving properly as it does to carve it. This is not far from being true, for unless all of the blemishes and scratches have been removed, any finish which is subsequently applied will but accentuate the defects instead of hiding them. So, in order to make sure that all blemishes have been removed, hold the carving at eye level, and with your back to the source of light, examine it carefully, as you slowly turn it about from one position to another.

Varnish, shellac, and lacquer are not used, since they greatly change the color of the wood. Since many of the woods are especially selected for certain color qualities, this would be highly undesirable. Certain kinds of wax, on the other hand, preserve the original color, and at the same time give all the protection that the carving needs.

California sugar pine has a very lovely, soft, creamy patina after three applications of the best obtainable grade of paste floor wax. Apply the first coat with a soft, clean piece of cloth. Let this dry for about twenty minutes, then rub until it shines. Repeat this process twice.

Walnut, mahogany, and poplar can be finished a great deal better by Simoniz. Three or four coats will be required for a good satin finish. The wax is applied to the wood with a damp cloth. Each application is allowed to dry, and is then polished vigorously. All excess wax must be removed from the eyes and other small inaccessible crevices before it gets a chance to become too hard. Once this finish has dried, it is almost impossible to smooth it down, or even to remove it.

A richer color is obtained on cedar if a coat of the floor wax is put on first, and then followed by several coats of automobile wax.

These finishes are easily and quickly applied, and they will bring out all of the hidden beauty of the natural wood without changing its color to any appreciable extent.

The colored figures, which are usually cut from pine or sometimes poplar, are painted after sanding, and then waxed. An inexpensive box of water colors will answer all color needs for this work. A thin coat of paint is first applied, followed by a smooth heavy coat. Let the painted figures get absolutely dry, then followed with three coats of floor wax as was done on the unpainted pine.